SAVING THE FUTURE
Agenda for Economic Development & Prosperity

Alex Otti

authorHOUSE®

AuthorHouse™
1663 Liberty Drive
Bloomington, IN 47403
www.authorhouse.com
Phone: 1 (800) 839-8640

Published by AuthorHouse 06/14/2016

ISBN: 978-1-5246-0787-6 (sc)
ISBN: 978-1-5246-0788-3 (hc)
ISBN: 978-1-5246-0786-9 (e)

Library of Congress Control Number: 2016907740

Print information available on the last page.

Contents

Dedication

In memory of my Parents,
Pastor Laz and Mama Rose Otti;
For values that endure.

Preface

As a young undergraduate of Economics at the University of Port Harcourt in the mid-1980s, the idea of occasionally weighing in on the intellectual arguments of the day occurred to me often. I always felt the urge to contribute to the pulsating exchanges and cerebral discourse on economic policies, especially in the area of development economics. But like any typical intellectual wannabe, the distance between wishing to write a book and actually writing it, can be a very long road. The challenges of an exacting career in the Banking and Finance industry which kept me engaged for the last two decades kept my ambition in check. But I never abdicated the intellectual's burden of periodic engagement. Even while I battled a hectic schedule at First Bank Plc, I still managed to moonlight as a guest lecturer at the Chartered Institute of Bankers. But it was the lecture circuit that provided me with the platform for sustained engagement. In 2013, Professor George Obiozor, chairman of Hallmark Newspaper Public Policy Forum, invited me to deliver a lecture on, "Saving the Future". Obiozor and many other guests who attended that lecture found it very fascinating and urged me to compile it into a volume for wider circulation. That paper which informed the title of this slim volume, was the spark that ignited this intellectual odyssey.

Like many other Development Economists who are engaged in the Nigerian system, I have often worried over our dysfunctional economy and the dangers it portends for the future generation. The perennial paradox of how Nigeria, a richly endowed country, can continue to wallow in avoidable poverty has never ceased to amaze and sadden me. The self evident truth is that Nigeria could do better. The billion naira question then is: Why not? Why is Nigeria a laggard, even if the statistics sometimes show differently?

I believe in a Nigeria that can succeed, a Nigeria that can achieve her true potentials as the giant of Africa and great hope of the black world. I came of age at a time of immense socio-economic and political challenges. My generation had great expectations of our country. Many of us embraced those challenges and rose to the peak of our careers. The central challenge of our generation, therefore, is to ensure that the doors of opportunities are kept open for the coming generation to actualize their potentials.

Saving the Future is my modest contribution to the vexed issue of how to ensure that Generation Next does not waste away. It examines the issues germane to national socio-economic development and illuminates a pathway to a better tomorrow. If the tone is occasionally apocalyptic and foreboding, it is merely a reflection of the permissive atmosphere of despair which an honest analysis of the Nigerian situation often engenders.

I owe a debt of gratitude to all those whose efforts made this book possible. Members of the MD/CEO's office at Diamond Bank Plc, Chuka Ofili, Ifeatu Onwuasoanya and Uche Odunze, former Chairman of the Board, the Obi of Onitsha, Igwe Nnaemeka Alfred Achebe, the Corporate Communications team, my colleagues on the Board of the Bank, and my publishers, Patrioni Books Limited, who worked tirelessly to meet the tough publishing deadline. Let me also thank my immediate family members: Chinwe, Ogbonaya Ezinwa and Pricillia Otti. It was their support that kept me going in the very difficult times.

If this book succeeds in ensuring a better world tomorrow for millions of Nigerian children and youths, then our various efforts would have been amply rewarded.

While thanking everyone who contributed to the success of this effort, I hasten to add that I accept full responsibility for whatever shortcomings there may be.

Foreword

I t is a rather pleasant task to write the Foreword to this important book by my good friend, Alex Otti. I have known him over the years as a friend and an accomplished banker and economist. Those of us who know him closely have always admired his calm and composed demeanour and his sterling leadership and professional standing in the banking and financial world. Alex Otti graduated with a First Class honours degree in Economics from the University of Port Harcourt and was the valedictorian of the Department as well as the Faculty of Social Sciences. He had his management and leadership education at some of the topmost business schools, among them Harvard, Wharton and Columbia.

Wherever he has worked, Alex Otti has left a mark of high accomplishment while earning the highest respects of his peers. In his last position as the Managing Director and CEO of Diamond Bank PLC, he was instrumental in turning around the fortunes of that organisation, repositioning it as one of the leaders in the industry. He has also served with distinction on the boards of several corporations within our country. A first-rate mind and a profile in courage and compassion, Alex Otti is not only one of the thought-leaders of our generation, he is a man that is truly blessed with the vision, wisdom and sagacity of King Solomon.

This book is a collection of lectures he delivered over several years at different forums. It is divided into eight chapters, namely: (1) A World Without Oil: Confronting the Realities of Emerging World Order; (2) Big Business and Nigeria's Economic Development; (3) Education and the Growth Imperative: A Time to Act; (4) Feeding the Future: Agriculture in the New World Order; (5) ICT and the Challenge of Sustainable Development; (6) Improving the Nation's Education System; (7) Nigeria, Your Glass is Half Empty; (8) The Squandering of Riches: How Nigeria wasted Her Oily Opportunity to Greed; (9) Saving the Future: The Challenge of a New Nigeria. Although dealing with different themes, the chapters have a common thread running through all of them: how to build a New Nigeria and how to salvage our common future.

Saving the Future is an urgent wake-up call to a new generation of leaders to rise to the historic challenge to save our nation and to retreat from the wasteful, destructive trajectory we have stumbled along over the decades. Alex Otti does not shy away from diagnosing our manifold national maladies: corruption, waste, poor governance, failure of the rule of law, the infrastructure deficit, weak property rights and the poor business environment. In his own words:

> (Some) 100 years from now where would we be? It is clear. If we do not reform, we will almost not make it. The nation would not exist. Its peoples or the survivors of those that survive would have been far-flung and scattered. There would be issues of identity and the apocryphal title used by the visionary Chinua Achebe would very sadly have been lived out in the epitaph: There was a Country!

At the heart of the national renaissance that he proposes is a commitment to returning to "the basics". The country needs to be rebuilt not in an *ad hoc* manner, but on "a structural, systematic, organised and efficient manner".

The work is littered with golden nuggets of insights from the world of business, high finance and economic science. The author demonstrates an uncommon understanding of world economics and the structural parameters of our twenty-first century integrated digital industrial civilisation. The author warns, for example, that our present reserves of oil of some 38 billion barrels are likely to last no more another 45 years while our gas reserves, estimated at 100 trillion standard cubic feet will last approximately 150 years. Given the trends in new energy technologies, over-dependence on hydrocarbon deposits is as foolhardy as it is dangerous. We must, therefore, diversify – and do so with the greatest urgency.

In conclusion, Alex Otti's agenda on *Saving the Future* is anchored on seven pillars: (1) addressing the imperatives of good governance and state effectiveness based on a culture of patriotism, selflessness and servant leadership; (2) reforming the bureaucracy and civil service to ensure that it is run by seasoned professionals with a sense of mission and destiny; (3) enhancing national competitiveness to ensure big business and small and medium-sized enterprises (SMEs can flourish); (4) revamping and modernising our physical infrastructure; (5) refocusing on education and skills; (6) rebuilding agriculture and ensuring food security, and (7) providing social welfare and social protection for the poor and vulnerable.

Like the great German statesman, jurist and man of affairs, Gottfried Wilhelm Leibniz, Alex Otti knows his differential calculus as he does practical business and the intricacies of statecraft and public policy. What is most memorable in my reading the manuscript is the spirit of optimism that suffuses every line and syntax of the work. I share this conviction with the author that Nigeria has the potential to become one of the leading nations of the twenty-first century if only we could put our home in order. "All is possible in this great country", he deposes, with passion and conviction.

I am persuaded that this book will prove to be an invaluable addition to the bourgeoning literature on Nigerian economics and public policy that will be of benefit not only to leaders but also to professional economists, researchers and students. I warmly recommend it to our emerging crop of enlightened leaders and patriots who love Nigeria, who seek its good and long for it to fulfill its manifest destiny among the nations.

Obadiah Mailafia D. Phil Oxon
Former Deputy Governor, Central Bank of Nigeria;
Chef de Cabinet, African, Caribbean and Pacific Group of States,
Brussels, Belgium

1

A World without Oil: Confronting the Realities of Emerging World Order

Overview

In April 2007, a television game titled, World without Oil (WWO), opened on Independent Television Service. It was an alternate reality game (ARG) created to call attention to spark dialogue about, plan for and engineer solutions to a possible near-future global oil shortage and post-peak oil. It was the creation of San Jose game writer and designer, Ken Eklund, and ARG veterans. World without Oil was presented on ITVS with funding from the Corporation for Public Broadcasting. The game's tag-line was, "Play it – before you live it." The game concluded on June 1, 2007.

The goal of the World without Oil game is to ask players to imagine a world reeling from a sudden oil shortage and describe how the crisis is unfolding where they live, and work as a team on simple and practical ways to adapt. By playing it out in a serious way, the game aims to apply collective intelligence and imagination to the problem in advance, and create a record that has value for educators, policymakers and the common people to help anticipate the future and prevent its worst outcomes. In sum, World without Oil invites people to, per its slogan, "Play it - before you live it". The game received rave reviews, several commendations and awards.

However, the game deals with a situation where oil is in short supply, for instance, through a sudden political action such as embargoes as we had in the past or some unforeseen circumstances. It was an acknowledgement of the importance of oil in the contemporary life of western economies and the growing power which oil producers now wield over them. The previous experience in 1973 was so unexpected and so traumatic to both the government and people of these societies that it remains a constant fear in their daily living.

But here we are looking at a situation where nobody especially in these same economies wants oil through a deliberate socio-economic and political policy. It is a reverse situation that the pains are on the producers rather than consumers as the game depicted. If the game served any purpose at all, it created an awareness of what can go wrong in the future that may have very deleterious implications for those affected. It was, therefore, more than a game because it expressed a creative imagination to live the future now: a preparation for tomorrow that will eventually come!

For us in this part of the world, it seems there is no tomorrow. And this explains the way we have exploited and expended our oil resources. Oil has conferred tremendous economic and political power, especially since 1973, on Nigeria and other members of the Organisation of Petroleum Exporting Countries (OPEC), a cartel of nine countries which controls about 60 percent of global oil export, and we now believe and think it will last forever. And for good reason, our present reserves of oil of about 38 billion barrels will last for 45 years while gas of 100 trillion standard cubic feet is estimated to last 150 years. What could be more reassuring as well as promising as this?

Unfortunately for us, the world is changing whether we like it or not, or are aware or not. Oil has been a double-edged sword – a curse and a blessing – to the world for about two centuries. The discovery of oil has brought about unimaginable technological development in the past century than all history put together. Oil has changed the way we live in the most unthinkable ways possible. Oil has taken man to the depth of the deepest oceans, to the greatest heights in space, and cut great distances to naught. But oil has also brought pains and misery, divided the world, devastated the ecology and endangers the earth and the future of mankind.

Oil, Nigeria's Economy and the Future!

To many people, the future of Nigeria and her economy is inextricably interwoven and inseparable with oil. After living on oil resources for the past 40 years, it has become practically inconceivable to imagine and think of the Nigerian economy without the major contribution of oil. Like the ostrich – or more historically, Nero, who fiddled while Rome burned – we have buried our heads in the sand oblivious of changes around us and the concerted efforts being made by the outside world to transit from oil. This explains the implacable and rigid positions our people hold on resource control and dependence on oil resources.

Our comfort in oil has immuned the nation and her leadership from recognising the threats posed by our continued and indeed increasing dependence on oil after 50 years, and taking the right and necessary steps to not only reduce such reliance but also confront the challenges of a world without oil. Tragically, the coming change is not about us and what we think. Instead, it is about the inexorable forces of nature and human development beyond the contemplation of any man or nation.

To perceptive and well informed eyes, the future without oil is already upon us and unless steps are taken to prepare and confront its emergence, its effects on our development will be more grievous than the damage done by oil. A world without oil is real and it is no longer whether it would be but when. It is no longer generations away; it is now in this generation.

For most of the world – both oil producers and consumers – the change from oil is being anticipated and preparations are being made for its arrival. Such awareness has removed any element of shock and surprise that usually accompany socio-economic and political change. Every social change creates role substitutions and consequently winners and losers. Transition from non-renewable to renewable energy will definitely change not only the way we do things but also the roles being played by the different actors.

In the particular case of oil, the emergence of non-oil energy will lead to the rise of new machines and technologies to replace oil-based machines as well as transfer the economic power from oil producers to the producers of the new energy source. For the oil producers, the consequence of changing from oil will have double negative impact: first, there will be the necessity of changing from old oil-based mechanisations, which would require heavy financial investment, and second, the loss of economic, as well as political, power, as producers of oil to the producers of non-oil energy. Both effects demand and impose financial burdens.

While the former impact is general in nature because it affects both producers and consumers alike, the second is exclusive to the producers who will suffer both economic and political power losses. Even at that, replacing oil-based machines and technologies is going to impose heavy financial burden on those who do not prepare adequately for it because every new energy source is progressively more expensive than the previous one it replaced. For instance, transition from wood and coal to oil involved expensive mechanical changes, even though the new energy is also less expensive. In the same vein, transition from oil to renewable energy will demand a lot of investment although the cost of the energy itself would be cheaper because of its renewable nature.

Most oil producers, especially those in OPEC, which are developing countries, are already conscious of this eventuality and committing everything necessary to mitigate the adverse impact of this technological and economic inevitability. They have not only diversified their economies into agro-industrial, human capacity and cleaner energy, such as gas, but are also investing in the economies of the prospective producers of the new energy to tap into the potential benefits to be accrued from it. For instance, the Arab world, which is the major oil producer, invests an annual average of $1 trillion in western economies. In fact, in 2013, UAE invested an incredible $800 billion in Europe alone. Indonesia, which is a middle level producer like Nigeria, is the third largest producer of rice and largest exporter of gas. Brazil, a non-OPEC nation (others being Russia, Brazil, Mexico and North Sea countries of Britain and Norway) and leader in the search for non-fossil energy, is already an industrialised economy. Iran, the second largest producer in OPEC, is almost a nuclear power which will reduce her oil energy dependency. The world largest producer of oil, US, does not export oil.

Why the Transition from Oil

There are several factors pushing for a quick change from oil. In previous transitions, economic factors had played major roles in the change from one energy source to another. But unlike the old era, other interests such as geo-politics and social factors have also come into play, making the present change most compelling and irresistible.

Historian Norman F. Cantor describes how in the late medieval period, coal was the new alternative fuel to save the society from overuse of the dominant fuel, wood:

> Europeans had lived in the midst of vast forests throughout the earlier medieval centuries. After 1250 AD they became so skilled at deforestation that by 1500 AD they were running short of wood for heating and cooking... By 1500 Europe was on the edge of a fuel and nutritional disaster, [from] which it was saved in the sixteenth century only by the burning of soft coal and the cultivation of potatoes and maize.

Petroleum emerged as an alternative to whale oil which had provided energy source hitherto. Whale oil was the dominant form of lubrication and fuel for lamps in the early 19th century. But the depletion of whale stocks by the mid-19th century caused whale oil prices to sky-rocket, setting the stage for the adoption of petroleum which was first commercialised in Pennsylvania in 1858.

High Cost of Energy

The high cost of the energy source compelled the search for an alternative. Human economic decision is a product of utility or value and cost. Every utility is measured in terms of its cost. When the value of a product is higher than the cost, there is great demand for the product. However, and conversely, when the cost surpasses the expected value, there is dissatisfaction and subsequently, a search for, and change to, a substitute. And cost considerations have always determined the appropriate source of energy.

High cost of a product is always a function of supply. Any product that is in demand usually has a challenge with supply and whenever supply is short of demand, price would be high. Those who depend on such product whose cost is sky-rocketing would not be content living with their fate. They characteristically seek change of the *status quo* by searching for an alternative. While producers are happy with high cost, consumers feel differently. Oil supply has been artificially and/ or monopolistically determined to regulate price.

Since the formation of OPEC, oil has become increasingly expensive as the price has been rising. Before its inception, oil price was less than a dollar. But afterward, it jumped to a negotiated $3 per barrel. Then there was the Middle East crisis of 1972 and the oil embargo on the West and first unilateral imposition of price by OPEC. Oil price went from $3 to as high as $18 per barrel. This brought stupendous wealth to OPEC at the expense of consumer nations. During the Iran-Iraq war in 1981, oil price rose to over $40 per barrel; it crashed during the glut of the 1980s but rose up again to over $40 during the Gulf War in 1990. In the past 15 years, oil price has hovered between $100 and $130, aided by global political crises, to the benefit of producers and discomfort of consumers. At a price above $55 per barrel, oil has lost its competitive edge to alternative energy.

Supply Challenge

Since the formation of OPEC, supply of oil has provided a particular challenge; for the first time, supply of such international product came under strict supply control. Before this time, the developed economies, through the Seven Sisters, namely, Standard Oil New York (Exxon Mobil), Standard Oil California and Standard Oil New Jersey (ESSO) (which three were formed following the forced break-up, by anti-trust law, of Standard Oil founded by billionaire J.D.

Rockefeller), Texaco, Royal Dutch Shell, Gulf and British Petroleum had controlled both the exploration and pricing of the product.

But economic nationalism in the Middle East and the rise of radical leaders in some of the oil producing nations, such as Ahmed Sukarno of Indonesia, Muammar Ghadafi of Libya and Saddam Hussein of Iraq, necessitated the need for a change of the old order where the Seven Sisters determined the supply and price of the product. This was a clear warning to the oil dependent world that they would have to pay a high price to satisfy their oil thirst.

However, it was the oil embargo on the West following the Middle East crisis in 1973 that sounded the clarion call for the inevitability of an alternative to oil. By that action, OPEC imposed considerable hardship and cost on the western economies, virtually grounding them. It exposed the dangerous state of an oil dependent global economy and threw up a new power bloc that was not part of the traditional stakeholders into international politics. Oil supply was no longer a function of the economic law of supply and demand but a political decision of the producers based on the international relations and equitable, rather than market, price.

Since the emergence of the Islamic Republic of Iran in 1979, the free flow of supply even in normal times, particularly to the US and the Far East, has been dependent on access to the politically sensitive Strait of Hamuz under the suzerainty of Iran. The Strait is a major thoroughfare from the Middle East, which is the main oil hub in global oil economy. A product loses not only its value but also becomes dangerous to rely on if its supply cannot be sufficiently guaranteed at all times. Without the non-OPEC producers, global economy would have been terribly jeopardised by the unpredictability of OPEC supply.

Besides the physical and political challenges of oil supply to the consumer nations, there is the increasing technological issue of getting it. Oil was first discovered and produced onshore (on the land) but production pressures and diminishing yields, and environmental degradation forced oil companies into the deep seas.

Deep sea exploration requires very high technology and sophisticated logistics which raise the cost of production and, by extension, the price, and reduce profit margin. It is also more difficult to manage and control and indeed more dangerous and more risky as witnessed in the oil spill off the Gulf of Mexico in 2011 lasting three months with over 100,000 barrels of crude oil daily spilled into the ecosystem.

A Political Power Bloc

The emergence of OPEC on the international political terrain created a power bloc that was alien in world politics. Before its formation, global political power used to be exercised by, and expressed through, military leadership and economic dominance. Before the last century, several European powers, such as Spain, France and Holland, had played dominant political power roles in international relations on account of their military prowess, which conferred economic advantage on them. Britain was the last of such powers that controlled many colonies including the Americas, which she eventually lost in 1783.

Since the end of World War II, this fact has been demonstrated by the existence of the United Nations Security Council which has five permanent members who are the most powerful nations in terms of both military and economic strengths. These are the US, Russia, China, UK and France. By all standards, these are world powers which won the world war and became by right the global custodians of political power and decision making. These powers determined global peace, security and social order. The exercise of this power imposed on them enormous responsibility in terms of contributions in both human and material resources in the exercise of this mandate. There are some common characteristics among these world powers, namely, they

a. are advanced industrial economies;
b. are militarily strong and indeed, nuclear powers;
c. are economically wealthy;
d. had once been global leaders in their own individual rights;
e. are also politically mature, and
f. also won the last world war.

Generally, international politics is usually a function of history and tradition, military power and economic strength. They all have these and they decide what happens in the system.

But the rise of OPEC changed this political equation and global power balance. Here were poor, backward and recently independent countries imposing themselves on global power loop and deciding the direction of political direction by virtue of their control of the energy resource of the world. It gave them power without responsibility and detracted from the conventional application of diplomacy (based on negotiations and consultations, compromises and collectivism in the use of force) as the norm in international relations. With OPEC, unilateralism and threat of force became the first resort.

Oil Embargo

The effects of the oil embargo were immediate. OPEC forced the oil companies to increase payments drastically. The price of oil quadrupled by 1974 to nearly $12 per barrel. This increase in the price of oil had a dramatic effect on oil exporting nations, for the countries of the Middle East who had long been dominated by the industrial powers were seen to have acquired control of a vital commodity. The traditional flow of capital reversed as the oil exporting nations accumulated vast wealth. Some of the income was dispensed in the form of aid to other underdeveloped nations whose economies had been caught between higher prices of oil and lower prices for their own export commodities and raw materials amid shrinking western demand for their goods. Much was absorbed in massive arms purchases that exacerbated political tensions, particularly in the Middle East.

This control of a vital commodity became known as the "oil weapon" which came in the form of an embargo and cutbacks in oil production from the Arab states to select industrial governments of the world to pressure Israel during the fourth Arab-Israeli War in October 1973. These target industrial governments included the US, UK, Canada, Japan and the Netherlands. In retrospect, the purpose of the embargo, as perceived by these target governments, was to sway their foreign policies concerning Israel towards a more pro-Arab position by threatening to cut off exports of Arab oil, and that in altering their policies, the Arab states would respond by again allowing their purchase of more oil. The Arab states selected their target governments to emplace their embargo, mostly affecting the European Common Market countries and Japan with an eventual 25 percent oil cut in production. However, in all five cases, there did not appear to be a dramatic change in policy making as envisioned by the Arab states.

Also, within the US concerning the economic impact at the macro level, direct correlations have been drawn between the rise in oil prices and economic recessions. "Oil price shocks", referring to disruptions in the production and distribution of oil, that result in the increase of oil prices, "have been held responsible for recessions, periods of excessive inflation, reduced productivity, and lower economic growth".

The effect of the Arab embargo had a negative impact on the US economy by causing immediate demands to address the threats to US energy security. At the international level, the price increase of petroleum disrupted market systems in changing competitive positions. At the macro level, economic problems consisted of both inflationary and deflationary impacts of domestic economies. The Arab embargo left many US companies searching for new ways to develop expensive oil, even in the elements of rugged terrain such as in hostile arctic environments. The problem that many of these companies faced was that finding oil and developing new oil fields usually required a time lag of five to ten years between the planning process and significant oil production.

OPEC member-states in the developing world withheld the prospect of <u>nationalisation</u> of the companies' holdings in their countries. Most notably, the Saudis acquired operating control of <u>Aramco</u>, fully nationalising it in 1980 under the leadership of <u>Ahmed Zaki Yamani</u>. As other OPEC nations followed suit, the cartel's income soared. Saudi Arabia, awash with profits, undertook a series of ambitious five-year development plans, of which the most ambitious, begun in 1980, called for the expenditure of $250 billion.

Other cartel members also undertook major economic development programmes.

Meanwhile, the shock produced chaos in the West. In the US, the retail price of a gallon of gasoline (petrol) rose from a national average of 38.5 cents in May 1973 to 55.1 cents in June 1974. State governments requested citizens not to put up <u>Christmas lights</u>, with <u>Oregon</u> banning Christmas as well as commercial lighting altogether. Politicians called for a national gas rationing programme. President Nixon requested gasoline stations to voluntarily not sell gasoline on Saturday nights or Sundays; 90 percent of owners complied which resulted in lines on weekdays.

The embargo was not uniform across Europe. Of the nine members of the <u>European Economic Community</u> (EEC), the Netherlands faced a complete embargo, the Uk and France received almost uninterrupted supplies (having refused to allow the Us to use their airfields and embargoed arms and supplies to both the Arabs and the Israelis), whilst the other six faced only partial cutbacks. The UK had traditionally been an ally of Israel and <u>Harold Wilson</u>'s government had supported the Israelis during the <u>Six-Day War</u>. But his successor, <u>Edward Heath</u>, had reversed this policy in 1970, calling for Israel to withdraw to her pre-1967 borders. Members of the EEC had been unable to achieve a common policy during the first month of the Yom Kippur War. The Community finally issued a statement on November 6, after the embargo and price rises had begun. Widely seen as pro-Arab, this statement supported the Franco-British line on the war and OPEC duly lifted its embargo on all members of the EEC.

- The price rises had a much greater impact in Europe than the embargo, particularly in the UK (where they combined with strikes by coal miners and railroad workers to cause an <u>energy crisis</u> over the winter of 1973/1974, a major factor in the <u>change of government</u>). The UK, Germany, Italy, Switzerland and Norway banned flying, driving and boating on Sundays. Sweden rationed gasoline and heating oil. The Netherlands imposed prison sentences for those who used more than their given ration of electricity. Edward Heath asked the British to heat only one room in their houses over the winter.

A few months later, the crisis eased. The embargo was lifted in March 1974 after negotiations at the <u>Washington Oil Summit</u>. But the effects of the energy crisis lingered on throughout the 1970s. The price of energy continued increasing in the following year, amid the weakening competitive position of the dollar in world markets.

It was a situation the big powers were, and are still, not enamoured of but had to live with for as long as it would last. It was an unwelcome and unwholesome challenge to the world political and economic order and ranking, threatening global peace and security. It was a bad and unacceptable development that had no immediate solution. But a solution must of necessity be found because the political and military powers of the big nations were in mortal jeopardy without resolving the threat posed by this new power bloc whose views and interests were politically diametrical and indeterminate but predominantly anti-establishment, and wholly different from the prevailing world view of the international system. This is clearly demonstrated in the current face-off between the West and Russia over Ukraine. Russia's intervention in Ukraine and Europe and US impotency in dealing with the situation is a function of Russia's power over Europe as the dominant supplier of its energy needs. Russia could cripple Europe by turning off the gas pipes, practically reliving the World without Oil game.

Environmental Activism

The dominance of oil in world economy also brought in its wake the rise of environmental activism against its devastation on the ecosystem and the ozone layer. Oil exploration is environmentally hazardous. Oil spills destroy both agricultural and aquatic life, and poses great health challenges to the people. The oil economy has the tendency of ruining the traditional lifestyle of the people and forcing them to abandon their natural means of livelihood.

Oloibiri, the birthplace of oil exploration in Nigeria, has since been abandoned by both the oil companies and the communities because of the environmental devastation. Again, the Ogoni agitation, which consumed environmentalist Ken Saro Wiwa, is a derivation of the fate of Oloibiri. Even the 2011 BP oil spill in the Gulf of Mexico, which gushed out 100,000 barrels of crude daily for three months before the damage was fixed, has left that US coast of Missouri impoverished and deserted three years after.

For several decades, environmentalists had drawn global attention to the incalculable damage being perpetrated by oil firms especially in the Third World to the irritation and annoyance of the political and business leaders of the developed economies. However, scientists in developed countries also began to warn that too much carbon emission, a by-product of oil combustion, has depleted the ozone layer, exposing the earth to dangerous atmospheric hazards such as scorching heat and ultraviolet radiation. Also, for a long time, they too were ignored through a conspiracy of silence by the oligarchy.

However, in 1980, the first global conference on the future of the Earth took place in the tourist city of Cancun, Mexico, to deliberate on the challenges confronting our world and ways to tackle them. For the first time, global attention was focused on the challenges and threats of oil exploration and utilisation to sustenance and human survival. It marked a breakthrough for the activists and scientists engaged in saving our world. This was followed later by the Beijing and Rio de Janeiro conferences. A fallout of these conferences was the reluctance of developed countries, particularly US and lately China, to put a timeline on the transition to alternative energy. However, such US opposition has begun to thaw as research reveals breakthrough in alternative energy.

Common Types of Alternative Energy

Historians of economies have examined the key transitions to alternative energies and regard the transitions as pivotal in bringing about significant economic changes. Prior to the shift to an alternative energy, supply of the dominant energy type had become erratic, accompanied by rapid increases in energy prices, as illustrated in the following examples:

Coal as an Alternative to Wood

Historian Norman F. Cantor describes how, in the late medieval period, coal was the new alternative fuel to save the society from overuse of the dominant fuel, wood:

> Europeans had lived in the midst of vast forests throughout the earlier medieval centuries. After 1250 they became so skilled at deforestation that by 1500 AD they were running short of wood for heating and cooking... By 1500 Europe was on the edge of a fuel and nutritional disaster, [from] which it was saved in the sixteenth century only by the burning of soft coal and the cultivation of potatoes and maize.

Coal Gasification as an Alternative to Petroleum

In the 1970s, President Jimmy Carter's administration advocated coal gasification as an alternative to expensive imported oil. The programme, including the Synthetic Fuels Corporation, was scrapped when petroleum prices plummeted in the 1980s. The carbon footprint and environmental impact of coal gasification are both very high.

Alcohol as an Alternative to Fossil Fuels

In 1917, Alexander Graham Bell advocated ethanol from corn, wheat and other foods as alternative to coal and oil, stating that the world was in measurable distance of depleting these fuels. For Bell, the problem requiring an alternative was lack of renewability of orthodox energy sources. Since the 1970s, Brazil has had an ethanol fuel programme which has allowed the country to become the world's second largest producer of ethanol (after the US) and the world's largest exporter. Brazil's ethanol fuel programme uses modern equipment and cheap sugar cane as feedstock, and the residual cane-waste (bagasse) is used to process heat and power. There are no longer light vehicles in Brazil running on pure gasoline. By the end of 2008, there were 35,000 filling stations throughout Brazil with at least one ethanol pump.

Cellulosic ethanol can be produced from a diverse array of feedstock and involves the use of the whole crop. This new approach should increase yields and reduce the carbon footprint because the amount of energy-intensive fertilizers and fungicides will remain the same, for a higher output of usable material. As of 2008, there were nine commercial cellulosic ethanol plants in US States.

Second-generation biofuels technologies are able to manufacture biofuels from inedible biomass and could hence prevent conversion of food into fuel. As of July 2010, there is one commercial second-generation ethanol plant, Inbicon Biomass Refinery, which is operating in Denmark.

Other Alternative Renewable Energy

   a. Solar energy is the use of sunlight as energy. Light can be changed into thermal (heat) energy and electric (light) energy.
   b. Wind energy is the generation of electricity from the wind.
   c. Geothermal energy is the use of the Earth's internal heat to boil water for heating buildings or generating electricity.
   d. Nuclear binding energy uses nuclear fission to release energy.
   e. Hydrogen is burned and used as clean fuel for spaceships and some cars.

Enabling Technologies

Heat pumps and thermal energy storage are technologies which use energy sources that normally cannot be obtained. Also, heat pumps have the advantage of leveraging electrical power (or in some cases mechanical or thermal power) by using it to extract additional energy from a low quality source (such as sea or lake water, the ground or the air).

Thermal storage technologies allow heat or cold to be stored for periods of time ranging from diurnal to interseasonal, and can involve storage of sensible energy (i.e., by changing the temperature of a medium) or latent energy, e.g., through phase changes of a medium (i.e., changes from solid to liquid or vice versa), such as between water and slush or ice. Energy sources can be natural energy (via solar-thermal collectors or dry cooling towers used to collect winter's cold), waste energy (such as from HVAC equipment, industrial processes or power plants) or surplus energy (such as seasonally from hydropower projects or intermittently from wind farms). The Drake Landing Solar Community (Alberta, Canada) is illustrative. Borehole thermal energy storage allows the community to get 97 percent of its year-round heat from solar collectors on the garage roofs, which most of the heat is collected in the summer. The storage facilities can be insulated tanks, borehole clusters in substrates ranging from gravel to bedrock, deep aquifers or shallow pits that are lined and insulated. Some applications require inclusion of a heat pump.

Renewable Energy *vs.* Non-Renewable Energy

Renewable energy is generated from natural resources such as sunlight, wind, rain, tides and geothermal heat, which are renewable (naturally replenished). When comparing the processes for producing energy, there remain several fundamental differences between renewable energy and fossil fuels. The process of producing oil, coal or natural gas fuel is a difficult and demanding process that requires a great deal of complex equipment, physical and chemical processes. On the other hand, alternative energy can be widely produced with basic equipment and naturally basic processes. Wood, the most renewable and available alternative energy, burns the same amount of carbon it would emit if it degraded naturally.

Ecologically-Friendly Alternatives

Renewable energy sources, such as biomass, are sometimes regarded as an alternative to ecologically harmful fossil fuels. Renewables are not inherently alternative energies for this purpose. For example, the Netherlands, once leader in the use of palm oil as a biofuel, has suspended all subsidies for palm oil due to the scientific evidence that their use "may sometimes create more environmental harm than fossil fuels". The Netherlands government and environmental groups are trying to trace the origins of imported palm oil to certify which operations produce the oil in a responsible manner.

Regarding biofuels from foodstuffs, the realisation that converting the entire grain harvest of the US would only produce 16 percent of her auto fuel needs and the decimation of Brazil's CO_2 absorbing tropical rain forests to make way for biofuel production, has made it clear that placing energy markets in competition with food markets results in higher food prices and insignificant or negative impact on energy issues such as global warming or dependence on foreign energy. Recently, alternatives to such undesirable sustainable fuels are being sought, such as commercially viable sources of cellulosic ethanol.

Relatively New Concepts for Alternative Energy

Carbon-Neutral and Methanol Economy

Carbon-neutral fuels are synthetic fuels (including methane, gasoline, diesel fuel, jet fuel or ammonia) produced by hydrogenating waste carbon dioxide recycled from power plant flue-gas emissions, recovered from automotive exhaust gas or derived from carbonic acid in seawater. Commercial fuel synthesis companies suggest they can produce synthetic fuels for less than petroleum fuels when oil costs more than $55 per barrel. Renewable methanol is fuel produced from hydrogen and carbon dioxide by catalytic hydrogenation where the hydrogen has been obtained from water electrolysis. It can be blended into transportation fuel or processed as a chemical feedstock.

The George Olah carbon dioxide recycling plant operated by Carbon Recycling International in Grindavík, Iceland, has been producing two million litres of methanol transportation fuel per year from *flue* exhaust of the Svartsengi Power Station since 2011. It has the capacity to produce five million litres per year. A 250 kilowatt methane synthesis plant was constructed by the Centre for Solar Energy and Hydrogen Research at Baden-Württemberg and the Fraunhofer Society in Germany and began operating in 2010. Its upgrade to ten megawatts was completed in autumn, 2012.

Audi has constructed a carbon-neutral liquefied natural gas (LNG) plant in Werlte, Germany. The plant is intended to produce transportation fuel to offset LNG used in their A3 Sportback g-tron automobiles, and can keep 2,800 metric tons of CO_2 out of the environment per year at its initial capacity.

Other commercial developments are taking place in Columbia, South Carolina, Camarillo, California and Darlington, England. Such fuels are considered carbon-neutral because they do not result in a net increase in atmospheric greenhouse gases. To the extent that synthetic fuels displace fossil fuels (or if they are produced from waste carbon or seawater carbonic acid, and their combustion is subject to carbon capture at the *flue* or exhaust pipe), they result in negative carbon dioxide emission and net carbon dioxide removal from the atmosphere, and thus constitute a form of greenhouse gas remediation.

Such renewable fuels alleviate the costs and dependency issues of imported fossil fuels without requiring either electrification of the vehicle fleet or conversion to hydrogen or other fuels, enabling continued compatible and affordable vehicles. Carbon-neutral fuels offer relatively low cost energy storage, alleviating the problems of wind and solar intermittency, and they enable distribution of wind, water and solar powers through existing natural gas pipelines.

Nighttime wind power is considered the most economical form of electricity power with which to synthesise fuel because the load curve for electricity peaks sharply during the warmest hours of the day. But wind tends to blow slightly more at night than during the day. So, the price of nighttime wind power is often much less expensive than any alternative.

Algae Fuel

Algae fuel is a biofuel which is derived from algae. During photosynthesis, algae and other photosynthetic organisms capture carbon dioxide and sunlight and convert them into oxygen and biomass. The benefits of algal biofuel are that it can be produced industrially, thereby obviating the use of arable land and food crops (such as soy, palm and canola) and that it has a very high oil yield as compared to all other sources of biofuel.

Biomass Briquettes

Biomass briquettes are being developed in the developing world as an alternative to charcoal. The technique involves the conversion of almost any plant matter into compressed briquettes that typically have about 70 percent the calorific value of charcoal. There are relatively few examples of large-scale briquette production. One exception is in North Kivu, in eastern Democratic Republic of Congo, where forest clearance for charcoal production is considered to be the biggest threat to Mountain Gorilla habitat. The staff of Virunga National Park have successfully trained and equipped over 3,500 people to produce biomass briquettes, thereby replacing charcoal produced illegally inside the national park, and creating significant employment for people living in extreme poverty in conflict affected areas.

Biogas Digestion

Biogas digestion deals with harnessing the methane gas that is released when waste breaks down. This gas can be retrieved from garbage or sewage systems. Biogas digesters are used to process methane gas by having bacteria break down biomass in an anaerobic environment. The methane gas that is collected and refined can be used as an energy source for various products.

Biological Hydrogen Production

Hydrogen gas is a completely clean burning fuel. Its only by-product is water. It also contains relatively high amount of energy compared with other fuels due to its chemical structure,

$$2H_2 + O_2 \rightarrow 2H_2O + \text{High Energy}$$
$$\text{High Energy} + 2H_2O \rightarrow 2H_2 + O_2$$

This requires a high energy input, making commercial hydrogen very inefficient. Use of a biological vector as a means to split water and, therefore, produce hydrogen gas, would allow for the only energy input to be solar radiation. Biological vectors can include bacteria or more commonly algae. This process is known as biological hydrogen production. It requires the use of single-celled organisms to create hydrogen gas through fermentation. Without the presence of oxygen, also known as an anaerobic environment, regular cellular respiration cannot take place and a process known as fermentation takes over.

A major by-product of this process is hydrogen gas. If we could implement this on a large scale, then we could take sunlight, nutrients and water and create hydrogen gas to be used as a dense source of energy. Large-scale production has proved difficult. It was not until 1999 that we were able to even induce these anaerobic conditions by sulphur deprivation. Since the fermentation process is an evolutionary back up, turned on during stress, the cells would die after a few days. In 2000, a two-stage process was developed to take the cells in and out of anaerobic conditions and, therefore, keep them alive.

In the last ten years, finding a way to do this on a large-scale has been the main goal of research. Careful work is being done to ensure an efficient process before large-scale production. However, once a mechanism is developed, this type of production could solve our energy needs.

Floating Wind Farms

Floating wind farms are similar to a regular wind farm. But the difference is that they float in the middle of the ocean. Offshore wind farms can be placed in water up to 40 metres (130 ft) deep, whereas floating wind turbines can float in water up to 700 metres (2,300 ft) deep. The advantage of having a floating wind farm is to be able to harness the winds from the open ocean. Without any obstructions such as hills, trees and buildings, winds from the open ocean can reach up to speeds twice as fast as coastal areas.

Alternative Energy in Transportation

Due to steadily rising gas prices in 2008 with the US national average price per gallon of regular unleaded gas rising above $4 at one point, there has been a steady movement towards developing higher fuel efficiency and more alternative fuel vehicles for consumers. In response, many smaller companies have rapidly increased research and development in radically different ways of powering consumer vehicles. Hybrid and battery electric vehicles are commercially available and are gaining wider industry and consumer acceptance worldwide. For example, Nissan USA introduced the world's first mass-produced electric vehicle, "Nissan Leaf". A plug-in hybrid car, the "Chevrolet Volt", also has been produced, using an electric motor to drive the wheels, and a small four-cylinder engine to generate additional electricity.

Making Alternative Energy Mainstream

Before alternative energy becomes mainstream, there are a few crucial obstacles that it must overcome. First, there must be increased understanding of how alternative energies work and why they are beneficial. Second, the availability components for these systems must increase. Third, the pay-off time must be decreased. For example, electric vehicles and plug-in hybrid electric vehicles are on the rise. These vehicles depend heavily on an effective charging infrastructure such as a smart grid infrastructure to be able to implement electricity as mainstream alternative energy for future transportations.

Implications for Nigeria

Why then should Nigeria be concerned? And why are our leaders not bothered in the least? Nigeria is Africa's largest producer of oil and the tenth in the world with 2.8 million barrels per day (bpd) production quota or 2.7 percent of global output, although her highest production output in recent time is about 2.3 million bpd and a proven reserve of about 38 billion barrels, which may last 45 years and a gas reserve of 0 trillion scf that will last over 150 years. In 2011, Nigeria earned $53 billion with an output of 2.2 million bpd and $43 billion with 1.9 million bpd in 2012. Oil and gas contributed 97 percent of total exports, 74 percent of government revenue, 16 percent of GDP and 94 percent of foreign exchange. Our dependence on oil is total.

So, in general estimation, Nigeria still has a grace period of 45 years to exploit her oil and eternity to use gas. To officialdom, there is time for the music to go on. Intermittently, officials of government remind us about the dangers of our sole reliance on oil and the need to diversify the economy. But they do very little to change the situation. Instead, what happens is mindless wastage of the resources from oil by those at various levels of government without regard to future repercussions. Most of them believe there is still time. But in actual fact, time is running out and we are already too late to the party.

While we may have oil reserves that could last 45 years, the oil companies and the consumer nations no longer have that luxury of time and are preparing to dump oil as the major energy source of the world as soon as practicable. All the factors, as already mentioned, are coming together to force a transition sooner than later. The US, the world's largest consumer and major buyer of Nigeria's oil at 53 percent of total output, has become self reliant in oil production and no longer imports from us, which has affected overall revenue – although China has replaced it. But it is a momentary reprieve as would be shown later.

The world powers, particularly the US, are doing everything to ensure that political and economic powers are retrieved from oil producing countries to reorder the international political system on the traditional single power centre that determines global political outcomes. In the past 15 years, energy cost has remained dangerously high which eats precariously into the living standard of the people of the consumer countries. The cost of developing new technologies and risk of exploiting from deep water has become prodigious that alternatives are becoming more attractive.

Also, growing agitations by communities and environment-alists have created moral question for both oil companies and consumer nations about their continued dependence on oil which is posing a danger to the very survival of man and the planet. Above all, the 2011 Gulf of Mexico oil spill, which has devastated huge portions of the US coastline, has brought home the reality of the dangers oil exploration and exploitation to man and the environment. The damage has been incalculable. Again, the opposition to restrictions to, and penalty on, the use of oil by the traditional vested interests such as the advanced economies and big oil corporations, is thawing, as transition to alternative energy becomes more realistic and practicable.

So, should Nigeria be concerned? In the article, "The World Our Grandchildren will Inherit,"
Daron Acemoglu says that

> Prediction about the future is often a vehicle for clarifying the challenges ahead and because it often extrapolates from experience, it also gives us an opportunity to take stock of the trends that have shaped our age.

He outlines some trends that will play out in the future which will directly affect Nigeria. Some of these trends are higher standard of living, sweeping technological growth and widening gulf between the rich and poor countries, among others. According to him, higher standard of living, like Keynes predicted in 1937, will be driven by new technologies that would strive to improve comfort and convenience by reducing costs of living. The second trend is that the new technologies will seek better, simpler, more environmentally friendly and more cost effective ways of doing things and living. According to him, the next phase of technological growth will be improving on, and removing areas of, present challenges and cost. And oil is a major part of that.

The third trend is a natural consequence of this development. Because this technological revolution will be led by the already rich countries who are investing in research and development today, they will continue to be richer in future as the rest of the world will depend on their technology to get by. Here are some specific implications for Nigeria.

Socio-Economic and Political Crises

With Nigeria's wholesale dependence on oil as the main source of her revenue, drop in revenue as a result of the inevitable transition from oil to alternative energies portends a fearsome socio-economic and political danger of a cataclysmic nature for the nation. With an estimated population of 300 million by 2025 at a growth rate of 3 percent, Nigeria may become the third most populous country in the world, after China and India. Without oil or even a reduced ratio of oil contribution to her revenue, the social threat from economic dislocation can only be imagined. Unemployment will double, investment in social facilities will drop, social discontent and violent protest will increase, and political instability will fester. Anarchy and Hobbesian state of nature will be our existential condition. And the reason is simple. Nigeria, in the past 50 years of oil exploitation, has not strategically invested the proceeds and diversified the economy. The gas sub-sector, which has greater promise because of its cleaner and more enduring and larger reserve, has been largely undeveloped, leading to the current challenges with electricity generation.

Agriculture has been totally abandoned. Present efforts to revive the sector, though highly commendable, is still a far cry from what is needed. Nigeria is now a net importer of food, which compounds her social situation because a nation that cannot feed herself would only be a slave to others. For instance, Nigeria imports 2.3 million metric tons of rice at the cost of ₦420 billion annually making her the largest importer of rice in the world. It is estimated that in 20 years at the present population growth rate, Nigeria will need 35 million metric tons of rice to feed her people. And without revenue from oil, hunger and starvation will be the first and immediate challenge.

Education provides the link to any transition from the old to the new by creating the stock of knowledge and technological base that can aid such transition. But it requires the right priority and investment to make this happen. In Nigeria, the education sector has been neglected, lacks focus and direction, with inappropriate programmes and objectives. The future belongs to technology in all its ramifications and without appropriate education priority and infrastructure, technological development would be impossible. As the nation is today technologically dependent, so it shall be in future. The future is what we do today and we have made the choice by doing little or nothing to ensure a different future for the nation.

Reverse Technological Development

Nigeria is making effort to consolidate her technological mastery of the oil sector. But major research and developments are moving toward alternative energy. The US and Brazil are leaders in the alternative energy development and everything is being put into it to accelerate its full commercialisation and replacement of fossil energy. Civilisations, empires and economic systems are displaced while still at their apogee. As Karl Marx put it, every civilisation contains the seed of its destruction. Fossil energy may be the dominant energy source today but its reign is over and its undertakers are just at the door.

Some may argue that this is scare-mongering and the reign of oil is not about to end. May be so! Oil may still have few years to provide revenue for the country. But like everything that has a beginning, its end is sure and soon. It is only countries that embrace this reality and begin to plan and prepare for the eventuality, will play a role in the coming economy without oil. As already stated, Nigeria should focus more on developing her capability in gas production by investing more in it. Gas is going to outlive oil because it is cheaper and more environmentally friendly. Without the technology and investment for alternative energy, gas may provide an immediate succour to oil. So, even long after oil, gas may still be required as energy source.

Perpetuation of Dependency

Most Nigerian intellectuals attribute our poor socio-economic and political performance since independence to what is generally referred to as neo-colonialism and dependency syndrome. This describes a situation where former colonies of the West still depend on, and are controlled by, their former colonial masters through some economic and political structures that perpetuate the old relationship. To some extent, this may be so. But pushed to its logical conclusion, this position attempts to absorb and exonerate post-independence leaders from the responsibility of changing their circumstances. This is not only irresponsible, but defeatist and escapist. It assumes that we are merely a victim of a treacherous and exploitative world economic system that is designed to promote the interest of the rich.

Nothing can be farther from the truth and this subject of oil eloquently illustrates this paradox. Nigeria has produced oil for over 50 years without maximising its potential. Other countries like Saudi Arabia, Indonesia and other Gulf states, to mention a few, have taken the pains to plough back the proceeds of oil into developing the economy. But Nigeria, on the other hand, has literally frittered away her oil revenue in ostentatious consumption and corruption. According to the World Bank, Nigeria has earned about $800 billion from oil since 1970 with little to show for it.

While the world is moving in one direction – alternative energy and gas – Nigeria is standing idly and doing nothing to move with the trend. Brazil, the main leader in alternative energy, is an oil producer. In fact, her oil company, Petrobras, has become active in Nigeria. Yet, they are also working toward a world without oil. The implication of this is simple: transition to alternative energy will perpetuate Nigeria's dependence on other countries for not only her energy need as we do today where the country exports crude oil and imports refined products, but also on investment and technology as it also is now.

History, Marx once said, repeats itself: first as a tragedy and second as a parody or farce. History is about to repeat itself in this regard. But this time, there will be nobody to blame but ourselves. Our future is in our hands to decide and direct. And whatever it becomes is our making. Dependency is a very expensive relationship. It is never in the interest of the dependant.

Conclusion

Some people may say that we have little to worry about: that oil will remain a priced commodity for some time to come especially in the near future, and that we need not bother much with the future because the future will take care of itself. And they may be right. But what do we have to lose by taking precaution? Already, our present station in the global economic system is parlous and degrading. We have become the dumping ground of all exporting countries, importing virtually every-thing under the sun because we have oil money and have neglected everything else.

Enlightened self interest demands that we do something to change our situation and guarantee the future prosperity of our children. The good book says the righteous leaves an inheritance for the children. What legacy will this generation bequeath to those coming after. It is only wise to do so, because the world will not get better economically.

2

Big Business and Nigeria's Economic Development

Introduction

The role of big business in national prosperity creation has been a debate theme among many scholars for decades. The argument has always transcended the issue of output generation and resultant prosperity but straddles a thin line comprising the role of big business in welfare enhancement. One undeniable fact in the entire debate is that big business has become particularly important in this era of globalisation in which smaller firms tend to be directly exposed to throat-cutting competition with global companies and other imports.

In spite of this, small and medium-scale enterprises (SMEs) or small businesses are mostly propagated by several policy decision makers as solution to unemployment and poverty. This is true to the extent that there is a corresponding policy effort to push for the growth and development of big businesses and/or the transition of small businesses to big ones, as the actual contributions of SMEs put together to overall size of national output is usually quite low relative to the share of big business. For example, a close look at the Gulf Cooperation Council's (GCC) programmes and policy initiatives aimed at developing SMEs and encouraging them to compete for government contracts, show that while SMEs in the GCC countries represent more than 90 percent of the private sector and employ over 70 percent of the private labour force, their contribution to the GDP of these countries is less than 30 percent. The reason is straightforward to understand: SMEs are concentrated in less profitable, less capital-intensive and low-technology sectors. Usually, they pay lower wages and produce less per employee. Members of the GCC are Bahrain, Kuwait, Oman, Saudi Arabia and UAE.

Big business, however, has been a major power behind national and global prosperity through its income and technology-transfer effects on smaller businesses. Where there is abundance of big businesses that are making good profits, then the effect would be more widespread and results in "big business revolution". In fact, high economic growth without large companies is virtually impossible. This is because the positive sides of the capacity of big business in reaping higher market shares by concentrating on core business, being able to establish global brands, possessing capacity for high density research and development (R&D) and IT technology investment, as well as easier accessibility to financial resources, are cascaded down the socio-economic ladder thereby increasing income and employment. Imagine how many businesses and families that are tied to the continued survival of the Dangote Group. Unofficial estimates of the supply/value chain show that the Group sustains at least 3,000 other businesses. In addition to this, there is enough evidence to show that big business can promote economic development by enhancing the value of a country's exports. They are also inevitable in informal regional integration within national economies. The simplest example here would be the establishment of regional distribution centres or mini-plants across the country. They also play pivotal roles in the creation of comparative advantages in product specialisation.

In general, the importance of big firms in the process of economic development is less contested. Various economists have shown how big business in the US and Germany has contributed to these countries' economic growth. A number of analysts have provided ample evidence regarding the importance of large firms in generating innovation, entrepre-neurship and subsequently economic development. From a slightly different angle, other economists have shown that more turnover (less stability of their rankings) in top business in a country is positively correlated with faster growth of per capita domestic product and productivity.

Differing Perspectives

There are myriads of different views regarding the position we hold on the developmental role of big business. The difference in the view is palpable in the notion that small business should be promoted in solving the problems of high unemployment and poverty that have co-existed in many developing countries. But existing data show that encouraging the growth of big business appears to be the best solution.

As an example, a study was conducted by the International Labour Organisation (ILO) on the relationship between economic development and the level of small businesses. The outcome shows that in highly productive countries such as the US and UK, small businesses constitute only about 9 percent of the entire businesses. In the newly industrialising countries like Taiwan, Singapore, South Korea and Malaysia, the share of small businesses in the aggregate portfolio of businesses is about 25 percent. However, small businesses comprise about 60 percent in poorer countries in Africa, Latin America and Asia.

This observation suggests that small business have not been the focal point for improving national productivity in the developing countries. Self employment and small businesses are individualistic work settings. Thus, when individuals produce on their own, total production is lower than when people work in large groups. In effect, therefore, big companies enjoy linkage effects or economies of scale. But such economics complement the efforts of a myriad of small-scale suppliers and vendors and tie up into a kaleidoscope of economically efficient activity.

Specialisation at work is most apparent in big business. The concepts of division of labour and specialisation developed by Adam smith (1776) helps us to appreciate this point better. Adam Smith observed that making the flat-head sharp-end pin involved 18 steps. When an individual carried out all the operations, the person produced 20 pins per day. However, when ten people were employed to share the operations, they produced 48,000 pins per day, an average of 4,800 pins per person per day. The major lesson from this illustration is that working in groups or in a collective of small firms in large organisational settings improves productivity and hence enhances prosperity.

Data from the US Census Board (2005) indicate that the bulk of net new jobs are created by firms with less than 20 employees. However, it has been observed that these net new jobs were difficult to reconcile with the fact that over the same period, small firms' share of total employment actually fell. Whatever the case, it is important to note that although the US data on new job creation is possibly true because the US has myriads of very large firms whose survival invariably gives life to small ones. In other words, small enterprises provide critical inputs to large firms.

As big business expands, managerial challenges result in tons of outsourcing while the number of embedded businesses grows as well. Also, in spite of new jobs created by small businesses, evidence suggests that large firms offer higher wages than small firms. Fringe benefits, ranging from health insurance and retirement benefit to paid holidays and vacations are also associated with large firms. Similarly, large firms tend to pay higher wages. What this implies is that for economies to grow in a loathly manner, there must be a proper rise of small and large enterprises to increase employment, support R&D as well as provide competitive economies of scale and size.

There is the notion in some quarters that small businesses are more innovative than big companies based on the fact that small businesses are less bureaucratic (Instagram, for example), that they operate in more competitive markets, and that the incentives to carry business activities is stronger than in large firms. But this assertion, together with the notion that large firms are too big and bureaucratic to make significant innovation, is not totally true. The cost of undertaking R&D is huge and usually takes large sales volume before it could be recovered.

Large firms generally have better access to external financing and so at times show stronger tendency to either innovate themselves or buy the innovation of smaller companies. Increasingly, firms have greater capacity to undertake several R&D projects in a diversified portfolio. Iwuagwu (2011) points out that "goodwill" is a factor that places large or big firms in more strategically advantageous position than smaller firms. Large firms tend to have an established reputation and name recognition which make it easier to growing trend. Therefore, large firms often take advantage of innovations through production and sales. In addition, having a large number of employees, which is more likely in large firms, facilitates better division of labour and the provision of solutions to problems.

Furthermore, many of the largest firms operate in industries in which only a few firms operate or dominate the market. For the most part, these firms do not compete with one another on the basis of price, but rather on the basis of quality and product differentiation. Given this market structure, large firms may, therefore, have strong incentives to innovate even though in Nigeria, their effort at adaptability has been slow.

Conceptual Clarifications

A number of yardsticks have been put forward to identify a big business. For example, American public officials provide a list of 280 American industrial enterprises with assets of $200 million or more each. Another standpoint proposes 1,000 employees as a possible benchmark for classifying big business. Some US analysts have suggested a yardstick of 10,000 employees and/or a share capital of £2 million before 1914, £3 million in the late 1920s and £5 million in the mid 1950s. Big business does not just occur in manufacturing industry as has been perceived in some quarters. On the contrary, it is a wider concept that includes firms from both the tertiary (in particular banking, insurance and public utility companies), the secondary and the primary sectors (the extractive industries).

Big business includes large-scale operations undertaken through vehicles other than integrated firms – various types of loosely or tightly knit, *ad hoc* or permanent business groups (including holding companies, financial syndicates, cartels and others) as well as independent financiers. In that respect, size, including the scale of financial transactions in certain undertakings, rather than organisational forms (level of integration and diversification, separation of ownership and control, managerial hierarchies), could be seen as the key elements in describing big business.

The Central Bank of Nigeria defines small and medium enterprises in Nigeria according to asset base and number of staff employed. Cottage/micro-scale businesses are those whose total cost, including working capital but excluding cost of land, are not more than ₦1 million and a labour size of not more than ten workers. Small-scale businesses are those whose total cost, including working capital but excluding cost of land, are over ₦1 million but not more than ₦40 million and a labour size of between 11 and 35 workers. The Federal Ministry of Industries defines a medium-scale enterprise as any company with operating assets of less than ₦200 million and employing less than 300 persons. Anything outside of these classifications can be considered a fairly big business.

Big Business and the Prosperity Trajectory

We are of the strong opinion that the mechanism through which big business transmits economic prosperity tends to be largely through its enhancement of economic activities of other businesses within its value chain. Typically, big businesses seen to have fairly long value chains with reasonable number of embedded services. Our experience at Diamond Bank indicates that each of these in turn has their own smaller value chains that are ultimately supported or given life from big business operations (see Fig. 2.1). Despite the importance of SMEs, one's experience as a banker suggests that large business does not only bring managerial and technological innovations, it also contributes significantly to output, income, additional investments and international trade.

Fig 2.1: Big business wealth creation trajectory

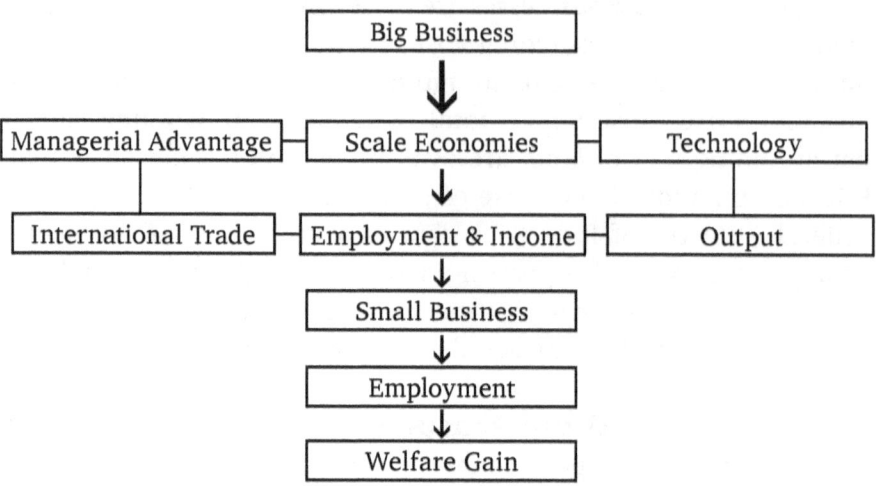

In spite of the lingering debate about the small business-big business dichotomy, big business still forms an integral growth driver for smaller entrepreneurs. Small business tends to handle the distribution chains of bigger entities. In addition to this, the interaction between small and big businesses usually leads to new knowledge, technological and managerial innovation transfers. These transfers rub off positively on the small business groups. Cumulatively, these positives come together to orchestrate income growth, financial stability, know-how and innovativeness that should, in our view, all lead to sustainable business prosperity

In getting the Nigerian entrepreneurial architecture right, we believe, the presence of big business should bring with it, not only economies of scale but also managerial and technological innovations which small companies can directly or indirectly benefit from. Economies of scale result in increased output and employment as well as increase in trade flows. In addition, employment is also created through retail distribution chains of products and services which are picked up by small businesses to augment the wealth creation effect of big enterprises. All of this translates into overall growth in the wealth of a nation. This suggests that if the behemoth dances, the entire economy dances along.

The Big and the Small

From the discussion so far, it is obvious that although big business is the key driver, there is a symbiotic relationship between big and small businesses which is important for the sustainability (local entrepreneurship) and by extension, the development of the Nigeria economy. The realisation of this fact by the government of UAE in 2012, for example, led to the signing into law of a bill that requires government bodies to allocate 5 percent of their budget for goods and services provided by small businesses.

When small business interacts with big business, they make changes that improve their organisational structures, management practices and operations. These changes lead small companies to upgrade their technologies, increase their efficiency and, most importantly, become financially stable (Badal, 2010). Small business also creates employment and income opportunities that sustain the demand for the products of big firms. An acquaintance once remarked that "a big firm ignoring a small firm is like a sunflower spurning a butterfly".

Big business tends to spend huge amounts of money seeking intermediate product inputs for their operations. They also outsource such services as landscaping, cleaning, logistics, software development, food services, etc, which are essentially provided, in most instances, by smaller firms. In fact, a research carried out by the Centre for an Urban Future which involved nearly 200 small businesses in the US shows that seven in every ten small businesses increased in revenue and size within two years of becoming part of the corporate supplier of larger organisations. This huge success comes from the fact that small firms are more flexible in providing innovative products and services to meet corporate needs. They are quicker in delivering services locally which saves cost for big firms. In his book, *How Large Corporations can spur Small Business Growth,* S. Badal identifies four specific ways in which big business can help small business to grow, namely,

Talent Identification and Support

Identifying top performers among small businesses based on talent and operational readiness is the first important factor. Once big companies have identified these small efficient businesses, they can provide mentorship to the talented entrepreneurs through supply development programmes.

Provide Financial Help

Small business needs support to meet large corporation's needs. A loan from a corporation or a community development institution could help small businesses with the capital to scale up their operations.

Making the Procurement Process Transparent

Getting information on business procurement process might be a hurdle to small businesses if the information is not presented in a simple manner. Big businesses are good at doing this.

Simplifying the Application and Selection Process

To ensure that high quality small businesses are selected for business relationship with big corporations, it is important to make the selection process more accessible and straight-forward. Big companies oftentimes use a single application, thereby making paperwork less burdensome.

Cross-Country Case Studies

The United States

At the turn of the 19th century, business enterprises in the US operated on a small scale dominated by the merchant capitalist. Most manufacturing concerns were operated by an artisan who was assisted by one or two apprentices or by family members. In fact, the largest industrial concerns, iron foundries and shipyards, rarely employed more than 50 workers. But towards the end of the century, this changed dramatically for two major reasons.

First, the industrial revolution gradually spread from England, where the increased use of machinery and economies of scale gave rise to the factory system and era of large companies. Second, legal changes that made big business more attractive were introduced. The US changed her incorporation laws so that the simple payment of a fee, rather than a special act of the state legislature, sufficed to make big business creation easy.

By 1850, large corporations had become the preferred method by which to finance and organise a business. American merchant capitalists, whose investment interests were being outpaced by government-subsidised British firms, were attracted by the limited liability benefits of corporate investment and the substantial profits that large-scale production produced. The efforts of the bankers to accommodate these investors led ultimately to the creation of Wall Street, the capital market centred in New York City through which stocks and bonds could easily be bought and sold. This growing scale and scope of business activity resulted in major development in transportation, communication, distribution and production

The first modern big business enterprises in the US were railroads. The invention of iron rails, flanged wheels and steam locomotives allowed railroads to replace rivers, canals and roads as the dominant mode of long distance transportation. Huge amounts of capital were required to purchase and maintain the necessary land and equipment, and large corporations proved the best vehicle for raising such funds. Big business in the rail sector employed thousands of workers in hundreds of different locations doing dozens of different jobs. Large managerial staff, composed of professionally trained employees, was developed. Most of these workers only worked for a salary, owned little or no interest in the company and made career out of their specialty.

The rise of mass production in the early 20th century resulted partly from major development in transportation and communication and partly from the development of new technologies. Large companies were incorporated to raise the capital necessary to build huge factories and equip them with state-of-the-art machinery. Professional managers headed departments, each of which employed thousands of workers dedicated to purchasing, manufacturing, repair, shipping, sales and accounting.

At a point in time in the mid-1890s, the US Congress attempted to restrict the rise of big business due to the growing formation of trusts, cartels and trade associations. Ironically, this act aided the growth of big business. Although, trusts were prohibited from engaging in monopolistic practices, big business was not prohibited. So, several small companies merged to become giant companies in a bid to gain competitive advantage over bigger companies. As an example, American companies such as American Continental Tobacco, General Chemicals, International Harvester, National Biscuit, Union Bag and Paper, and the US Steel, controlled between 40 and 90 percent of their industry's market shares.

All in all, big business in the US had been responsible for the spate of industrialisation in the 19th and 20th centuries. Statistics show that over one-third of all manufactured goods produced in the US were made by one percent of US manufacturers. The economic changes resulting from the rise of big business were generally beneficial to consumers and investors. Big business contributed to substantial economic growth by developing new goods and services, often as a result of technological innovation that was beyond the capabilities of small enterprises to finance and exploit. They also created a number of modern business practices such as integrated operations, cost accounting and mass production.

Furthermore, big business created millions of jobs for unskilled and property-less workers, many of whom were immigrants, thereby enabling them to support their families. The new specialties and middle management positions created by the large corporations allowed intelligent and educated people of average means to improve their lot, both socially and economically at an unprecedented rate.

Big business in the 21st century has played pivotal role in helping the US government achieve her monetary policy objectives of reduction in employment. According to US Census Bureau (2009) which published statistics about business size, it was noted that in 2008, 20 percent of 7,601,169 establishments with payroll in the US were actually big businesses with 100 employees and above. Despite their slim proportion to total establishments, they are able to generate employment to 65 percent of total paid employees, as shown in Table 2.1. The table shows the employment position in the US and the role of big business in generating employment. It is seen clearly that the big firms actually provided jobs for the larger populace in 2008 where the annual payroll for firms with 500 employees and above was greater than the addition of other categories of firms.

Table 2.1: Employment size of firms

Employment Size	Firms	Paid Employees	Annual payroll($1,00)
All firms	28,952,489	120,903,551	5,130,509,178
Non-employer firms	21,351,320	n/a	n/a
Employer firms	7,601,169	120,903,551	5,130,509,178
Firms with 1 to 4 employees	3,624,614	6,086,291	232,062,907
Firms with 5 to 9 employees	1,056,947	6,878,051	222,504,912
Firms with 10 to 19 employees	667,463	8,497,391	293,534,352
Firms with 20 to 99 employees	705,430	20,684,691	774,589,335
Firms with 100 to 499 employees	359,902	17,547,567	706,476,693
Firms with 500 employees or more	1,186,813	61,209,560	2,901,340,979

Source: United States Census Bureau (2009).

South Korea

South Korea has witnessed an incredible transformation in the three decades spanning from the 1960s to the 1990s, evolving from an impoverished country to a developed high-income economy today. This remarkable turnaround was achieved through the development of big business and large-scale industrial conglomerates commonly called "chaebols" which literally means "business association". Chaebols are large multinational family-controlled conglomerates in South Korea which encouraged economic development through large business conglomerates. Examples of chaebols are Samsung, Hyundai, LG and Daewoo. Today, chaebols have become multinational powerhouses with global footprint. With this, South Korea boasts of an economy that ranks 15th globally in nominal terms and 13th in purchasing power parity terms.

Chaebols consist of a number of independent groups of vertically integrated firms. The industries these groups are involved in are completely unrelated to each other, the only common link being their ownership. In the 1970s and 1980s, the government selected certain chaebols to undertake projects and channelled funds for these projects from foreign loans. The government would guarantee repayment if for any reason the company was not able to repay its creditors. If additional loans were needed for these projects, domestic banks would make the loans. This was the case until the late 1980s when the chaebols became multinational businesses and were too large to remain under the control of the state.

Many chaebols had become financially independent and the government was no longer needed for credit and assistance. It was at this turning point in history that the chaebols began to have considerable economic and social influence in South Korea and in the new global market. The chaebols' supremacy in the Korean economy was evident in their expanding presence in the economy. The top 30 chaebols' contribution to the country's GDP swelled from 9.8 percent in 1973 to 29.6 percent by 1989. Further, by 1997, the 30 largest chaebols accounted for virtually half of the total assets, debts, sales and net profits of the corporate sector in the economy.

Fig. 2.2: Chaebol structure

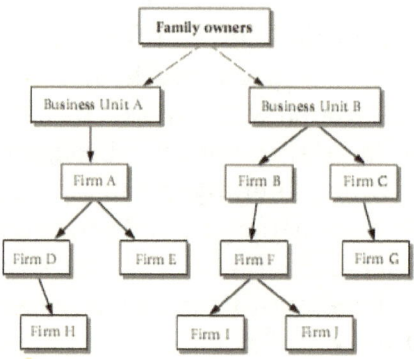

Source: Howard *et al* (2004).

Virtually all the sectors were dominated by chaebols as can be seen from Table 2.2 and each of them has an average of 54 subsidiaries. Their influence in the Korean economy is so great that the top five chaebols own 29 percent of the private sect or's total assets.

Table 2.2: Business areas of top five chaebols

Industry	Hyundai	Samsung	LG	Daewoo	SK
Automobile	*	*		*	
Aerospace	*	*		*	
Construction	*	*	*	*	*
Consumer Electronics		*	*	*	
Financial Services	*	*		*	
Machinery	*	*	*	*	
Oil Refinery	*		*		*
Petrochemicals	*	*	*		*
Semiconductor	*	*	*		
Shipbuilding	*	*		*	
telecom Equipment	*	*	*	*	
Telecom Services				*	*

Source: Emerging market spotlight.

Table 2.3: Chaebol influence in the Korean economy

	Total Volume	Top 5 Group (%)	Top 30 Groups (%)
Assets (billion won)	910,044	29.22	46.25
Liabilities (billion won)	736,584	29.79	47.94
Revenues (billion won	875,156	32.29	45.94
Employees (thousands)	21,048	2.7	45.86

Source: Phil-Sang Lee.

China

Four reasons can be identified for the rate of explosive growth of the private sector in China in the last 24 years. They are as follows:

1. the need to create jobs and to produce sufficient products to satisfy the diverse demands of the Chinese people.
2. The operational efficiency of the private sector was found to be much higher than that of the public sector, including state-owned and collective enterprises. The private sector's operation depended on self management and was charged with risk. So, there was no "free lunch" for this sector from either the central or local governments. The owner of the private firm had to work hard, manage effectively and innovate ceaselessly.
3. Government policies improved tremendously within this period which resulted in the rapid growth rate of the private sector than the other sectors.
4. During this past 24 years, the central and local governments supplied the conditions and policies conducive for developing the private sector. For example, the virtual privatisation of the agricultural sector led to massive boom of non-agricultural individuals. The private sector flourished and individual business activities and private entrepreneurial activities were upgraded and elevated. Some large-scale private enterprises (as large as state-owned enterprises in terms of overall assets and gross product) have been formed in China since then onward.

As Table 2.4 shows, the development of the private entrepreneurial activities has successfully pushed the entire national economy forward. During the period, 1991-2000, the average annual growth rates of private firms, private sector employment and industrial output, were 32.21 percent, 28.82 percent and 53.59 percent, respectively. The reforms in the financial sector accounted for major success of this private sector growth. City commerce banks and the presence of regulated money changers found their presence all over China to advance credit to the private sector. The enactment of laws that protect legal income and income distribution among factors of production further promoted and built confidence in private entrepreneurs leading to expansion in local capital investment. Formerly, private economy was termed a social evil and there was every attempt by the ruling communist party to eliminate any activity driven by profit motive.

Table 2.4: Private firm development, 1989-2000.

Year	Number ('000)	Growth (%)	Owner ('000)	Workforce ('000)
1989	91		210	1,426
1990	98	8	224	1,478
1991	108	10	241	1,598
1992	140	30	303	2,015
1993	238	70	514	3,213
1994	432	82	889	5,594
1995	655	52	1,340	8,222
1996	819	25	1,705	10,007
1997	961	17	2,042	11,450
1998	1,201	25	2,638	14,453
1999	1,509	26	3,224	16,498
2000	1,762	17	3,954	20,112

Source: Liu Y (2003). 'Development of Private Entrepreneurship in China: Process, Problems and Countermeasures.' In *Entrepreneurship in Asia: Playbook for Prosperity* (CD publication by the Maureen and Mike Mansfield Foundation Programme).

China Business Survey of 2013 found government policies and regulations as important drivers that continue to promote the growth and productivity of private business. From all the top executives that participated in the survey, only 19 percent found government regulations as severe constraints to their operations while most (not fewer than 90 percent) of the participants, however, described the relationship with government as key to business success. Although the primary source of finance for two-third of the sample remains self-financing, yet 50 percent of the participants are well-favoured by loans from banks.

The survey showed that thousands of businesses are actively in operation in China where over 40 percent are foreign-owned companies which belong to the medium and large categories; 38

percent of these foreign firms are capable of employing 300 to 9,999 people while 43 percent are capable of employing over 10,000 people. The huge employment capability of these companies has had impressive performance on their revenue growth.

Big Business in Nigeria

Achieving economic development through rapid industria-lisation has been a major challenge in Nigeria, and it has remained the primary focus of various administrations. Series of economic development policies have been advanced and comprise the import substitution strategy, indigenisation policy, structural adjustment programme (SAP), National Economic Empowerment Development Strategy (NEEDS), Seven-Point Agenda, Vision 20:2020, all in an attempt to ensure private sector growth. Virtually all the big businesses in Nigeria are multinationals, where the convergence of ideologies, tastes, fashion, technologies, easy capital and labour mobility, have made their presence in Nigeria inevitable. It is well known that nearly all the big players in the global oil and gas markets do business in Nigeria. Companies such as Shell, Agip, Eni and ExxonMobil have operated in the country for decades. Also, Nigeria has played host to many of the biggest pharmaceutical multinationals. At a point, some of them pulled out and those that remained were indigenised to become full Nigerian companies. These big companies are also increasingly involved in trade, banking and insurance.

Big business in Nigeria, as in other countries, exhibits a natural tendency to maximise their capacity and take advantage of economies of scale. Economies of scale are captured by very large companies in such a way that national economies are able to profit from lower costs and hence higher efficiency that in turn generates economic growth. They also have the tendency to successfully turn the fixed costs generated by their various R&D activities into positive productive effects.

Some economists have pointed out that large companies can reap higher market shares by concentrating on core business, establishing global brand, high density of R&D and IT investments and easier accessibility to financial resources. Big business in Nigeria is not left out in this global trend; even the indigenously owned large firms in Nigeria are also beginning to seek opportunities outside the national frontiers. Fig. 2.3 shows selected big companies in Nigeria from different sectors with foreign branches.

Fig. 2.3: Big business as a percentage of NSE

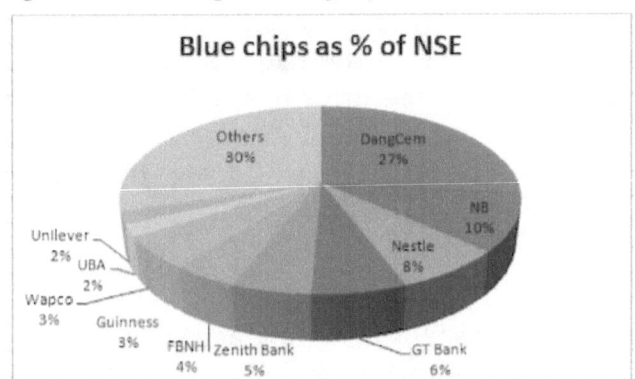

Source: Author's computation

Some specific roles played by big business in Nigeria include:

Big Business and Growth

The relationship between economic growth and the increasing number of large firms in Nigeria is noteworthy. Big business has been able to capture larger share of the Nigerian market in their respective production fields. Hence, they have increased their domestic production and the nation's GDP. For example, over the last 25 years, Nigeria has received over $300 billion in oil revenues, a sector dominated by international oil multi-national corporations. Also in 1965, Nigeria's oil revenue per capita was about $33. But this figure grew tremendously despite high population growth to $325 per capita.

Furthermore, the telecommunication sector, which is dominated by the big players in the telecoms world such as MTN, Globacom, Etisalat and Airtel, have also contributed to the growth of the nation's economy. According to Pyramid Research (2010), the total service revenue generated by the mobile operators in Nigeria increased significantly from \$135 million in 2001 to roughly \$7.0 billion in 2008. It is also estimated that mobile service revenue has grown from representing 1.2 percent of GDP in 2001 to roughly 4.2 percent of the country's economy in 2009.

Big players in other sectors of the economy such as in the manufacturing and services have also emerged, and they are significantly contributing to the nation's GDP. For example, the market value of the top ten firms in the Nigeria Stock Exchange is valued at ₦8.7 trillion, where Dangote Cement has the highest market share value with ₦3.3 trillion, followed by Nigeria Breweries at ₦1.2 trillion, etc, as depicted in Fig. 2.3.

Getting the Kids to Work

One of the spillover effects of large scope and scale economies enjoyed by large firms in Nigeria is the millions of jobs they have created for Nigerians. As an example, Nigeria's telecommunication industry has created jobs that rely on the distribution of mobile technology and services. This contribution takes the shape of employment beyond the telecoms operator ranks which they have achieved by enhancing entrepreneurship, productivity and other commercial skills. According to the Nigerian Communication Commissions, telecoms operators employed 8,000 people directly and around 3 million indirectly in 2008 (Pyramid Research, 2010). The indirectly employed includes, among others, vendors, PR agencies, call centre employees, security personnel, "umbrella people", street hawkers, phone ladies, etc.

Furthermore, the adoption of friendlier trade policies and some attractive investment incentives by the Nigerian government has attracted big international firms from several countries around the world which has brought about increased employment generation for Nigerians. There are, at least, ten Chinese big companies in Nigeria scattered over the various sectors of the economy.

Table 2.5: Ten major Chinese companies in Nigeria

Companies	Sector of Activities	Assets (USD Bln)	Employees	Investments in Nigeria
Sinopec	Oil and gas	152.8	373,375	Blocks OML 64,66,29% stake and operating rights to block 2, Nigeria-Sao Tome Joint Development
CNPC	Oil and gas	470.8	1.67 million; 80,000 foreigners	Licenses for OPL 471, 721, 732, 298
SEPCO	Electric power construction	38.6	19,756	Licenses for OPL 471, 721, 732, 298
CCECC	Const-ruction	2.17	70,000	Rehabi of Papalanto-Lagos express way, Athletes village, Ikot Akpaden-Lekki Free Trade Zone, Okoroette road,
CSCEC	Const-ruction, real estate	58.9	12,1500	Refinery
CNOON	Offshore oil and gas	13.8	21,000	45% interest in offshore exploitation licence, OML 130
Sinoma	Cement Engi-neering construction	2.9	9,000	In collaboration with Nigeria's Dangote Group for cement production line EPC project, 2008
CGC	Const-ruction	0.3	n/a	Kebbi Airport, Water supply project in Gombe, Sakke Dam
Huawei	Telecom	25	51,000	Network, handset
ZTE	Telecom	13	85,232	CDMA, handsets

Source: Egbula and Zheng (2011).

Welfare and Responsibility

Big business has empowered their communities by building trust funds that provide support initiatives in education, skill development, agriculture, small enterprise, adult literacy, etc. These support initiatives indicate the active commitment of these companies to sustainable business development. How-ever, it could be observed that enterprises that adopt this sustainable business policy as evidenced in their support initiatives to their host communities are majorly big players in the oil and gas, telecommunication and banking industries. These companies integrate sustainable development principle into their corporate social responsibility agenda in order to create a balance between economic, environment and social values.

Shell Petroleum Development Company (SPDC), for example, embarked on a series of projects and programmes as a way of implementing its corporate social responsibility programme. In 2012, Shell invested $103.2 million directly towards addressing social and economic development challenges in the Niger Delta region. The LiveWire Nigeria initiated by Shell has trained over 5,000 youth so far. Support for education in local communities also led Shell to invest $5.3 million on innovative scholarship programmes and the promotion of educational excellence and academic achievement (SPDC, 2013).

Furthermore, some banks have also dedicated some of their resources to corporate social responsibility. For example, Diamond Bank has spent millions of naira in the following areas commonly referred to as EEES, which are providing ease to the community through education, environment, economic empowerment and special (EEES) projects. Also, in 2013, many other banks in Nigeria committed to implementing their corporate social responsibility so as to impact positively on their communities. Obviously, all these engagements can be directly linked to the activities of the large Nigerian corporations.

Challenges Facing Big Business
Poverty

Nigeria boasts of one of the fastest-growing economies in the world with GDP growth rate above 7 per cent in the last ten years. Home to more than 170 million people, it is the most populous nation in

Africa and the largest concentration of black people in the world. The United Nations has projected her population could rise into the top three by 2050, potentially overtaking the US. In spite of her abundant riches in human and material resources, her foreign direct investment attraction has not been able to reach full potential. Big business already established in the country is seeking investment opportunities in neighbouring states due to the state of business environment in the country and the myriads of challenges of doing business in the country.

The World Bank ranks countries annually on the ease of doing business. It rates economies in relation to how easy it is to do business in each country. In the 2012 ranking, Nigeria was ranked at number 133 out of the 183 countries reviewed. Out of all the parameters used in arriving at the final ranking, access to electricity stuck out for Nigeria as she was ranked almost at the bottom of the pile at number 176. The reason for this poor ranking is coincidentally one of the major challenges that big business faces in doing business in Nigeria.

Insecurity

A major challenge facing big business in Nigeria has always been the political and national insecurity of the country. Nigeria has had a tragic history of conflicts and power struggles, being a country that consists of more than 500 different ethnic groups. Since gaining independence in 1960, Nigeria has had eight military governments, numerous civilian-led governments and experienced a 30-month civil war. Since the return of democratic dispensation, there has been an upsurge in political and civil unrest in the country, ranging from the problems of the Niger Delta to the Jos crises. More recently is the upsurge of the *Boko Haram* epidemic that has bedeviled the nation. This has not only affected and threatened the political sovereignty of the country, but also has damaging effect on the continuous existence of these blue chip companies in Nigeria. Billions of naira have been lost as a result of the calamitous damage done to lives and property by the *Boko Haram* scourge. Attempts have been made by the federal government to put a stop to the scourge. Still, we continue to experience the state of insecurity in the country which is dangerous to the continuous existence of big business in Nigeria and even the attraction of new ones.

Problem of Power Supply

Another major challenge facing big business in Nigeria has, over the years, been the shortage, or perhaps the epileptic nature, of power supply. Tons of hundreds of firms from different sectors of the economy, ranging from textiles to telecoms, beverages to banking industry, have been shut down due to the shortage of power supply. Big business now resorts to alternative forms of energy for their operation, which is ultimately reflected in the pricing of the firms' products.

Studies show that big business (manufacturing) uses over 40 percent of the profit on running operation fuelled by alternative power. If this additional income is not diverted in financing alternative power, saving and further investment will grow by 10-20 percent annually (MAN, 2012). More importantly is the fact that existing firms have been able to survive this power problem because they had built, over the years, monopolistic identities for themselves. New business coming into the country might not be able to survive this situation and as such drive away any further foreign investment inflow into the country. This is not particularly an interesting development if Nigeria intends to become one of the 20 most industrialised economies by 2020.

Lack of Infrastructure

Big business also faces serious infrastructural challenges in Nigeria. Today, there are little or no public (utility) enterprises that are functioning effectively. Most are either wound up or practically non-existence. This is the bizarre state that big business in Nigeria has been compelled to operate under. The road network is unbelievably terrible and this has aided the heavy congestion of traffic both on the metropolitan and the highways. This situation has not been particularly desirable for big business as most have to transport their products from their warehouses to the markets.

The rail system has been ineffective for a very long time, though attempts are being made to revamp it. The air transport system has also had its own challenges in recent time. Infrastructure is dilapidated and utility is practically non-existent, Big business winds up paying hugely in an attempt to provide alternatives for all these inefficiencies of the public sector and all this sums up in raising their cost structure which is not helpful for their profitability and continuous existence.

Corruption

According to **Paul Eze (2012),**

> Corruption is the hydra headed enigma that has prevented the nation from reaching the heights expected of it; it is something any business has to be aware of before stepping into business big time in Nigeria.

He further argues that businesses that are usually most affected by this scourge are the big construction firms, big conglo-merates, companies in the oil and gas sector, export firms and big joint venture firms. Being aware of the fact that you will bump into unscrupulous individuals who will demand unsolicited payments to get contracts, deals or licensing to establish new business or product line, will only help you know how to handle such issues when they come up because they surely will. This is challenging! According to the 2013 *Corruption Perception Index* of Transparency International, Nigeria was ranked 144th out of 146 countries, beating Bangladesh and Haiti to the last positions. An analysis of the anti-graft/anti-corruption laws in Nigeria shows that corruption will continue in spite of the laws because the perpetrators do not fear any consequences. With this caveat in mind, big business will find the country unattractive in spite of the profitability potentials the country possesses. So also is the withdrawal of existing big business. This is because of the time it took them to obtain licenses to start new investment or new product line due to an official wanting his hands greased. The implication of this will not only have devastating and calamitous consequences on the country's employment generation potentials, but also worsen the current unemployment situation in the country.

The Tax Man Cometh

One of the most contentious and debated subjects of fundamental significance to the economic life of not only big business, but also to the Nigerian economy, is the issue of multiple taxation. This has been one of the major challenges of big business over the years. They have been compelled to pay huge tax not only on varieties of bases, but also at each level of government. The exact number of "taxes" levied on big business seems to vary significantly between various tiers of government and "businesses may be subject to as many as 100 different taxes, charges, fees and levies, and in some instances taxed for the same event or asset" that are levied by the three ties of government (FIRS, 2008).

The impact of multiple taxation on competitiveness and, therefore, external integration, can be profound. In addition, the effect of multiple taxes on the transportation of products and consumer goods, in particular, impairs the integration of internal markets and the establishment of a fully integrated economic space within Nigeria, implying much broader economic and social impacts, including on poverty level. This situation has been particularly disturbing for big business in Nigeria because not only does it affect their short-run profit margins, but do also impede their long-run existence.

Experience with lending and business development shows that legal framework and enforcement environment is the single most important challenge big business faces in the country. Big business might and have survived in the face of the other challenges in Nigeria. But they may not be able to survive without an effective, efficient and non-partisan legal and regulatory environment and framework. The World Bank has ranked Nigeria 147th among the best places for doing business. It also ranks the country as the 122nd for best countries to start a business. The cause of Nigeria's low ranking is mainly due to the country's poor regulatory environment and other infrastructural issues where the country is ranked 185th out of 189 countries evaluated. The first African country on the list is Rwanda, ranked 32nd. This is damaging for a country regarded as the economic hub of the continent and a country with the most concentration of the black race in the world. The Nigerian legal system is "nothing to write home about". There have been issues of delay in adjudication of cases, contractual settlement delays, issues of corruption, political influence in the judicial system, etc. The regulatory environment is not investment-friendly and most of all, it is not one that favours big business. With these limitations in mind, the following policy recommendations can be drawn:

a. There is need for government to provide a policy environment that will allow big business to strive, as result has shown that big business in Nigeria still survives amidst political instability and infrastructural deficiencies in the country.

b. Investment-friendly macroeconomic policies should be well-articulated, formulated and vigorously pursued in order to enhance industrialisation-led economic growth and development of the country.

c. There is a serious need to attract more foreign direct investments especially in the sectors of the economy that have not been fully exploited. This will not only serve as a catalyst for economic growth, but also an avenue to diversify the production and export base of the economy.

d. Tax policy of the government should be geared towards encouraging big business by providing tax concessions, as this will help increase their profitability, expansion, employment and Nigeria's economic growth and development.

e. The energy sector is a principal driver of industria-lisation. As such, energy policies especially should be geared towards improving the supply of power and energy in the country. This will not only encourage foreign direct investment into the country, but also help improve the productivity of the real sector of the economy.

f. Due to the fact that big business can withstand shock and has survived irrespective of infrastructural deficiency of the country which has been the major factor hindering the growth of small business in Nigeria, short-term policy directed at improving the number of big business and expansion of existing ones should be formulated and vigorously pursued.

Ensuring Sustainability and Profitability of Big Business in Nigeria through the Private Sector and NGOs

Apart from the infrastructural, institutional and regulatory environment that the government has to put in place to promote the profitability and sustainability of big business in Nigeria, the private sector and the non-governmental organisations (NGOs) also have a role to play in achieving these objectives. These include:

Social Responsibility

Corporate social responsibility (CSR) is one of the ways which big business can employ to improve their profitability and sustainability in Nigeria. Social responsibility has been an avenue which big business uses to promote their corporate image by giving back to the society. Big business exists to make profit and that objective is not meant to change. However, what is required to change is the perception of the public towards them. The reality is that "no organisation" operates in isolation. There should be interaction with their employees, customers, suppliers and shareholders.

CSR has overall positive impact on society whilst making profit. There are a lot of benefits of big business in Nigeria can get by participating in corporate social responsibility. These include improving their corporate image, earning respect and building strong relationship with the public, attract investors and minimise risks. This can only help improve their profitability and sustainability.

Environmental Sustainability and Eco-Efficiency

In Nigeria, environmental realities are also driving corporate sustainability effort. There is little doubt that environmental issues, particularly climate change, are going to alter the regulatory and market landscape in the near future. Energy-efficient companies will be better able to navigate these regulatory changes and be better positioned to weather negative events like energy price spikes. This is a reality that big business in Nigeria must take with keen interest if they have any ambition of building a profitable and sustainable business. This is because environmental-friendly business derives enormous benefits from their contribution to environmental sustainability. It helps save money from reduced waste and increased efficiency, improves public relation, improves employee pride and morale, attracts motivated employees and investors and helps minimise risks, financial and otherwise, from the impact of climate change.

Compass Strategy

Developed and popularised by Unilever Nigeria Plc, compass strategy is a business strategy designed to help build a sustainable business for a long term and to find new ways to operate that do not just take from the society, but give back to the society. Captured in the company's "Sustainable Living Plan" programme, it spells out the company's vision and purpose and defines four pillars that will help to achieve them, namely, brand and innovation, market-place dominance, continuous improvement and people orientation. Other big businesses in Nigeria can also take a lead from this Unilever initiative to promote their corporate interest in the eyes of the public, as this could only help improve their profitability and sustainability.

Institutional Realignment

This is another medium which big business in Nigeria can employ to improve their profitability and sustainability. This involves matching the goals and objectives, as well as the missions and visions of the organisation to the regulatory environment. Big business does not operate in isolation. It operates and is guided by one form of regulation or the other. The more they internalise, align and realign the philosophy of their organisation to this institutional framework, the better it helps shape the direction of their profitability and sustain-ability.

Non-Governmental Organisations

Non-governmental organisations (NGOs), such as the trade unions, civil society, etc, can also help by:

a. putting pressure on big business to perform their corporate social responsibility by monitoring the activities in terms of giving back to the society;
b. helping to ensure that big business strictly follows environment regulation. This is done by ensuring big business contributes to environment sustainable through the management of their waste;
c. helping to improve the profitability and sustainability of big business by putting pressure on big business and ensuring that their products conform to required standard;
d. helping to enlighten and sensitise the public on the responsibility of big business towards them, as well as their responsibility toward big business within their environment.

Big business offers better, secure and high paying jobs when compared to small businesses. They contribute significantly to technological, managerial and marketing innovations. So also do they contribute significantly to R&D. Therefore, the government is encouraged to ensure the proliferation of large firms in Nigeria by providing the necessary logistics in terms of basic infrastructure, sound policies and regulatory environment, restructuring the entire tax system that will enhance the competitiveness of not only the big business, but also the Nigerian economy at large.

3

Education and the Growth Imperative: A Time to Act

Introduction

Without any equivocation, education is accepted the world over as an engine of growth that is very important in achieving development in every society. Accordingly, many societies endeavour to focus on their critical elements of access and quality. In the book, *Building a New Nigeria: The Right Approach*, J. Dangana argues that the scope and extent by which a nation can maximise her potential is hinged on the size of the space created by such a nation for the education of her citizens. We cannot but agree with him. Evidence, the world over, also attests to this fact. The most developed nations in the world today are also the highest net spenders on the educational circuit.

The development of a given society, therefore, can be said to depend on the primary recognition that education is a pillar that other sectors rest on. Therefore, education, as a foundation for human development, is a critical success factor in the development process.

According to the United Nations Educational, Scientific and Cultural organisation (UNESCO), the global consensus for enhanced educational development the world over is derived from the fact that a more educated society would invariably translate into higher rates of innovation, higher overall productivity through the ability of firms to introduce new and better production methods, and the faster introduction of new technologies.

Growth has, therefore, increasingly become a focus of debate in discussions about the development of educational policy and practice around the world. However, the way in which we achieve this is much more challenging. The word "growth" simply connotes concepts such as evolution, advancement, expansion, increase, production and prosperity. In the context of economic development, growth is a product of the combination of endogenous and exogenous threats or opportunities which prepare and drive a nation into greater prosperity whereas the opposite of growth relates to terms like decline, stagnation and underdevelopment.

Indeed, the impact of education on the economy of any nation is a very direct one. This is because it entails the nurturing of societal talent for sustainable growth and development. In getting the best out of the process, however, there is acknowledged decades of stagnation and lack of progress in the nation's educational space. And one preliminary observation we must make even now is that while education is central to the development of any society, it is indeed a quite costly enterprise that requires huge resources to deliver. This is most important to note given that as national resources remain scarce, education competes with other socio-economic needs of the society for public resources. The challenge then is how to find all the resources that must be put into education and to ensure that they are also well disbursed and utilised in a structured, monitored and goal-driven framework.

On the positive side, it is to be recalled that there have indeed been several waves of positive and incontrovertible growth in the history of modern education in Nigeria. One of the first was in the immediate aftermath of our contact with the West which brought in its wake the missionary schools and later government and community schools. Next was the revived boom in the nation's educational development process that was chiefly instigated by the transfer of political power in the immediate pre-independence era to indigenous political players at the regional level. From Western Nigeria, through Eastern Nigerian to Northern Nigeria and later the Mid-Western Nigeria, there was progressive competition amongst the new kids on the block to prove that they were worthy of their new and increased leadership roles and the educational sector was a first and primary beneficiary.

Currently, and in the wake of decades of dereliction of duty by successive governments, private entrepreneurs and religious bodies again have stepped in to fill some of the gaps in the system. But the verdict is that though some of the inputs and outputs from this have not been very complimentary, it could have been generally worse if the private and mission schools were not there. What is needed then is for a comprehensive revamp of the nation's educational infrastructure in such a way as to ensure that there is put in place a global plan that would match the imperative of education with the ultimate value and benefit that education would bring to the educated, the community and the nation.

In his study, "Education and Economic Growth in Nigeria: An Analytical Approach," J. Odeleye asserts that it is generally accepted that education influences development and *vice-versa*, although the linkage is usually perceived in different magnitudes. The significance of education in increasing the productive capacity of people is clear from the fact that education equips human resources with the needed knowledge, skills and competencies which would make them functional and contribute to the all-round development of the nation.

Consequently, the link between education and economic growth is predicated on the assumption that education, especially at the higher level, makes individual workers more productive and leads to the creation of knowledge, ideas and technological innovation. The crust of the matter remains that education is key to national development. No nation can achieve sustainable development without substantial investment in human capital because education raises people's productivity and creativity and promotes entrepreneurship and technological advancement.

Yet, the education system in Nigeria remains inappropriate to the need of the economy. In the prevailing 21st century economy, Nigeria still operates a 19th century education system, a system which, as accentuated by P. Osalor in a November 2013 piece in the *Vanguard* newspaper, gives much emphasis on the conventional classroom environment with much reverence for certificates for graduates who in most cases are trained to be job seekers as evidenced in the present high unemployment rate in the land.

Moreso, the technical vocational education and training (TVET) sub-sector is unable to respond to the changing labour market requirements due to its supply-leading orientation rather than demand following. TVET is offered at secondary schools and technical and vocational colleges aimed at the training of a lower and middle-level manpower base for accelerated development. The TVET programmes are teaching outdated skills using outdated curricula, machinery and equipment without significant link and involvement of the employers, especially the private sector. However, the recent initiatives of the National Board for Technical Education (NBTE) indicate a policy change directed at transforming the polytechnic curriculum to support the development of core competencies and generic skills so as to increase the chances of polytechnic graduates in dynamic labour market demands. This is a response to the need for demand-driven policies.

According to L.Y. Canete, the rapidly increasing unemployment situation has aggravated the worsening poverty and social problems with serious consequences to the economic growth of the country. Whereas education may be a vehicle that frees the poor from poverty, the trends in developing countries indicate that the poor are less likely to obtain basic education. Children of the poor are forced to stay out of school not only by factors of cost but also by the resultantly very low quality of education which paradoxically tends to suggest that it may perhaps be more valuable for them to drop out of school and pick up any menial jobs they can find rather than stay in school to get a sub-standard education that ultimately would not equip them with the aptitude and skills that the real sector requires.

Emerging from the trends in human development and great attention to education in developed countries, it is now widespread practice that a productive development strategy would be to raise the schooling levels of the population. This thinking provided the impetus for Education for All (EFA) and the United Nations Millennium Development Goals (MDGs) targets for education. The EFA goals are early childhood care and education, universal primary education, youth and adult learning, literacy, gender parity and quality. Similarly, the United Nations MDG targets relating to education emphasise universal basic education (UBE) as the pivot of educational development. This thinking is getting embedded in the planned sustainable development goals targets on education which are currently being formulated to succeed the MDGs.

Review of Related Literature

Education is a vital component of economic growth, the impact of which stems from human capital formation. It increases the productive capacity of people. The human capital theory regards education and training as a key element in human resource development in fulfilling a strategy of economic growth. The provision of formal education is seen as a productive investment in human capital. Indeed, researchers have long identified that about the most distinct feature of economic system is the growth in human capital. The absence of human capital may lead to heavy dependence on manual work and precipitate poverty. According to human capital theory, investment in education and training contributes directly to economic growth at the national or regional level. It further states that education and training will lead to advantages for individuals through improved earnings and career prospects. Others have also argued that education helps to supply the essential human capital for sustainable economic growth and also provide the key to poverty reduction and a major vehicle for promoting equity, fairness and social justice. These continue to be the focus of development institutions on education in developing countries. As a result, the foundation of most education reforms in these countries is anchored on the need to increase labour productivity and promote effective economic development and growth through expanded and improved education. It has also been posited that it is possible for poor countries to grow very rapidly if they make a major public commitment to raise the average level of schooling of the masses.

The macroeconomic implication of education on economic growth of a nation is well elucidated in growth literature. Indeed, this influence of education on economic growth encompasses at least three arguments:

1. Education increases the human capital inherent in the labour force which increases labour productivity and, thus, transitional growth towards a higher equilibrium level of output.
2. Education may increase the innovative capacity of the economy; the new knowledge on new technologies, products and processes promotes growth.
3. Education may facilitate the diffusion and transmission of knowledge needed to understand and process new information and to successfully implement new technologies devised by others which again promote economic growth.

It has also been stated that when estimating the effect of education on economic growth, the focus should be on how much students have learned while in school rather than counting how long students have been or sat in school. This is because some other commentators believe that years of schooling are an imperfect measure of human capital. The quality of the education system determines the educational outcome since the quality is mainly dependent on the efficiency of the education system, the quality of teaching and the educational infrastructure or the curriculum.

Many researchers have indicated that there is a significant relationship between investment in education and economic growth. Some of these studies have since confirmed that there is a long-run relationship between enrolment in the primary and tertiary levels of the educational pyramid and the average years of schooling with the resultant output per worker.

In a treatise titled, "The Growth Implications of Human Capital Investment in Nigeria," A.S. Bakare, employing vector auto-regressive error corrections mechanism, investigated the growth implications of human capital investment in Nigeria using data of investment on human capital and the GDPs between 1970 and 2000. The study shows that there is significant relationship between investments in human capital and economic growth in Nigeria.

Another scholar, R.O. Dauda, also carried out an empirical investigation on the relationship between investment in education and economic growth in Nigeria, using annual time series data from 1977 to 2007. The study which is titled "Investment in Education and Economic Growth in Nigeria: A Co-integration Approach" employs the notable Johansen co-integration technique and error correction methodology. The outcome of the empirical study also indicates that there is a long-run relationship between investment in education and economic growth.

In the broadest sense then, education, scholars say, is primarily an investment by the state for the continued existence, development and general welfare of her citizens. Besides national economic development, education is concerned with all aspects of national life including the economic, social, political, religious, ideological needs and aspirations of individuals. Therefore, it prepares an individual for a career in life.

Education in Nigeria: An Overview

Since independence in 1960, the Nigerian government saw in education the keys to social and economic development. Education, as the path to individual self improvement and national prosperity, inspired many countries to reform their educational systems to make learning relevant to the job market. The situation in Nigeria portrays inverse trends. Despite the sorry state of educational development in Nigeria, the young educated population is groomed without appropriate job skills. This calls for greater initiatives beyond traditional government schemes through an imaginative approach that will spur alliance for growth among business, government and the education system. Such collaboration will likely foster successful mechanism to align education systems with socio-economic demands of the country.

The inability of the government to match supply with demand of education and skills is a major concern for Nigeria. Indeed, education, as the engine of human capital, affects the drive for economic growth. According to UNESCO, it is generally agreed that expanding educational opportunities and access promotes economic growth. In Nigeria, like in most developing countries, the focus on access to education by all children overshadows attention to quality whereas the quality determines how well children learn and the extent to which their education translates into a range of personal, social and developmental benefits. Despite huge investment in education and, of course, large pool of educated population in Nigeria, the economic reforms in the country still rely heavily on foreign expertise or trained professionals, perhaps due to greater confidence in standards and quality of education obtained abroad.

The federal government's policies on education centre on two key areas: access and quality. Although education is on the Concurrent Legislative List, the local and state governments are mainly responsible for primary and secondary education while the federal government is more concerned with tertiary education. At present, Nigeria operates a free and compulsory Universal Basic Education (UBE) programme which is a nine-year schooling system and three-year senior secondary education. Additionally, a minimum of four years is required for university education and a minimum of two years and three years for National Diploma (ND) and National Certificate of Education (NCE) in polytechnics and colleges of education, respectively. According to Rufa'i, in terms of improving the quality of education delivery, the federal government targets comprise the construction and rehabilitation of infrastructure, provision of teaching-learning support resources, and recruitment, retention and capacity development of teachers at all levels. Furthermore, the federal government has reviewed the nine-year basic curriculum to meet national objectives. At the tertiary education level, the Minimum Academic Standards for Undergraduate was reviewed and the Basic Minimum Academic Standard (BMAS) was developed for postgraduate courses in universities. Also, teacher training curriculum has been reviewed to enhance the development of quality teachers. However, the federal government strategies for achieving its conceived education goals have not indicated concrete proposals from the state and local governments who have greater responsibility for primary and secondary education. Moreso, greater emphasis is given to quantity rather than quality of the education being provided by the government, because the governments at all levels seem to be more interested in contract awards for the construction of classrooms without serious concern for the quality of teachers, availability of instructional materials and discipline generally.

It is a fact that the education sector is not insulated from the general rot in the society. The sector is confronted with myriads of challenges, especially poor funding characterised by lack of infrastructure, poor quality, insufficient access, indiscipline and corruption. According to the Transformation Agenda of the Jonathan Administration, "one out of three eligible children is not in school due to problem of access and other socio-cultural factors". It also states that there is a challenge to access to higher education due to low carrying capacity of the institutions with adverse effects on development.

Since independence in 1960, Nigeria has been experiencing increasing expenditure on the provision of public education by governments at all levels. This is in accordance with the constitutional provision that put education on the Concurrent List. Moreso, with the continuous support of international development institutions such as the World Bank, greater emphasis is given to improving access to further education and training towards achieving Education for All (EFA) and the United Nations MDGs targets on education. The National Policy on Education (NPE), which came into existence in 1977 (revised in 1988, 1999 and 2004), stipulates that it is the responsibility of the government to provide pre-primary education, to promote training of qualified teachers and to ensure full participation of government and communities in pre-primary education. It is also the duty of the government to set and monitor minimum standards for early child education. Primary and secondary education prepares students for tertiary or higher education.

The National Policy on Education of 2004 prescribes a system towards achieving free education at all levels in Nigeria. It precipitated an unprecedented expansion of education provision which has unintended consequence in a phenomenal decline in the quality of education. Meanwhile, many children from well-off backgrounds began attending private primary and secondary schools to gain good foundation for admission into tertiary institutions. The present quality of education in Nigeria is comparatively poorer than what was obtainable under the colonial period and even during the first three decades of independence. The standards of education have degenerated to the level that parents are seeking education for their children in other countries. The decay in education is obvious looking at the standard of primary and secondary education as well as tertiary institutions, many of which operate more or less as glorified secondary schools in content and standard. Population boom has continued to exert pressure on governments to fund and deliver quality education through state managed public education system. Another major goal of the National Policy on Education is to equip every individual with the skill and job competency for gainful employment. This goal makes curriculum at every stage of formal education – primary to tertiary levels – to be geared towards participation and competencies. However, the National Summits on Education commencing from 2002 under the democratic governments indicate that, in the words of the writer and social commentator, Odia Ofeimun, "much of the thinking that went, and continues to go, into its implementation has no significant relationship to the goals". It is obvious that each summit on education crises proffered solutions that are incongruous with the need to create a national policy on education.

Despite the poor state of education in Nigeria, skilled young people are rapidly migrating to seek employment in foreign countries in the face of aging workforces in Europe and North America. This talent is largely from private education sector which emphasises the ability to pay school fees to the exclusion of the children of the poor majority in the society. This calls for more innovative ways of fostering the education of the poor. For example, the failure of government schools in India to provide the required quality education caused one-third of Indian children to attend private schools. This precipitated the policy which requires that a fourth of the seats in all private schools be reserved for the poor whose fees are subsidissed by the government.

Challenges of Access to Quality Education in Nigeria

The challenges of access to quality education or education for all are invariably dependent on resources available for education. Any policy framework aimed at pupils' enrolment in schools towards achieving 100 percent success must also take **cognisance** of funding sources, especially in developing countries where public resources are limited. UNESCO points out that greater access to education can be achieved through unprecedented refurbishing and building of classrooms in many countries. The disparity in access to qualitative education is discernible from increasing uneven growth largely due to inequality in geographical areas, urban and rural sectors and households or income groups.

Following political independence, most African countries view the development of education as basic element of achieving three major goals of producing a scientifically literate population, increasing labour productivity and producing knowledge to harness economic potential. These goals precipitated continuous governments' investments in education through sustained budgetary allocations and use of donor assistance. In Nigeria, investments in education permeate the entire educational system, from primary to tertiary levels, although the United Nations gives greater concern for basic education (primary and secondary) which is the major index for literacy. For example, the United Nations emphasises Universal Basic Education (primary and junior secondary) which remains the bedrock of any educational pursuit and the relevance of the private sector on education and more recently secondary education. However, the poor outcome of education in Nigeria has continually attracted serious attention of the policy makers, parents and employers. Despite her huge resources, Nigeria's literacy rate is still low at 61.3 percent (male 72.1 percent and female 50.4 percent - 2010 estimate) and the gross enrolment rate also is low. According to the data by UNICEF, one out of every four children of school age is out of school which is equivalent to about 10.5 million children with girls constituting the majority (FME Annual Report, 2012).

Primary and Secondary Education

Quantity and quality are two major components of educational development in any society. Whereas quantity is concerned with enrolment or number of citizens getting access to schooling within the shortest time allowed, quality is about how good or bad the products are. Quality assurance is the systematic review of educational programmes to ensure that acceptable standards of education, scholarship and infra-structure are being maintained. Quality assurance, thus, is a major challenge to educational planners and managers because quantity is easier to deliver than quality. The significance of the quality of education is further accentuated by **Ijaiya** who states that "education without quality is a waste and portent danger to both the beneficiary and the society". The state of education in Nigeria remains a serious concern to all: governments, parents, children and other stakeholders in education, including employers. The politicisation of education in terms of recruitment of unqualified persons to teach in primary and secondary schools and the admission of unqualified candidates, exacerbated the declining quality and wastage in the education system. This is characterised by factors such as high drop-out and failure rates, rampant examination malpractices, poor reading and writing skills among students at all levels.

Quality of education is about meeting standards and quality control is geared towards determining the extent to which a product meets that standard. According to **Cole**, quality control is essentially a system for setting standards and taking appropriate actions to deal with deviations outside the permitted tolerances. The pillars of quality assurance are predicated on class size, number and quality of teachers and instructional materials, as well as appropriate education environment. The pursuit for quality teaching as a vital aspect of quality assurance in education is imperative due mainly to the emergence of knowledge economy. The global competition for technically-skilled workers creates a national urgency to improve the educational system. Ayeni insists that the poor funding of education has remained the bane of quality assurance. Inadequate funding of education has precipitated the systemic malfunctioning of the inspectorate system. The breakdown of the inspectorate system poses serious challenge to quality assurance due to the attendant problems which revolve around poor teaching and learning that culminated into negative behaviours as manifested by large-scale examination malpractice and appalling performance of students in external examinations. These depict non-achievement of quality assurance in teaching and students' learning outcomes, especially in secondary schools. This is evident from the poor performance of students at the Joint Admissions and Matriculation Board (JAMB) Unified Tertiary Matriculation Examinations (UTME) examination and the post-UTME screening conducted by universities. The emergence of private schools or private education is often attributed to the continuous falling standards or quality of public schools because parents could not rely on the poor state of educational services for their children in the public schools, particularly at the primary and secondary schools levels. However, private schools need close monitoring to stem the abuse which is now commonly entrenched by corruption and bad business ethos. The menace of students from private schools with excellent senior school certificate examination (SSCE) results who could not pass the JAMB-UTME or post-UTME screening is a serious cause for concern.

The strategy adopted by many countries in addressing the issue of quality of education is decentralisation of school management system, particularly as a means of reducing wastage and ensuring greater quality, as quality control is exchanged for quality assurance. It should be noted that quality assurance is a preventive rather than a corrective measure. Achieving quality assurance requires greater accountability in school management system which transcend to the entire school management, including principals, teachers, parents, students and the society at large. Educational accountability is the backbone for quality assurance. The concept of reward and punishment is desirable in attaining excellence in service delivery. Accordingly, staff promotions, transfers and retirement should be linked to pupil achievement in schools which can be evidenced from routine monitoring and, indeed, performance at external examinations. It should, however, be noted that accountability requires an enabling environment because for effective and efficient management of the school system, there must be adequate funding that will guarantee instructional facilities for the teachers and the students. Whereas in the present circumstances, where Nigerian teachers work under difficult and unstable conditions such as inadequate teaching facilities, irregular and inadequate remuneration, underfunding of education and strikes, accountability is compromised. The delivery of quality education is the responsibility of all stakeholders which comprise policy makers, resource providers, policy implementers and students, as well as the community.

Effective quality assurance can be achieved through a two-pronged approach, namely, internal quality assurance by schools and external quality assurance mechanism by government inspectorate agencies. Internal quality assurance is achieved through school-based management, participation of parents and teachers, and self-evaluation by schools. The external quality assurance bodies created by government are responsible for the external quality assurance activities. These bodies are state universal basic education boards and senior secondary schools management boards for primary and secondary schools, respectively.

The challenges facing primary and secondary education in Nigeria revolve around issues of access and quality of education. In summary, the major challenges are as follows:

Responsibility and Control

Education being on the Concurrent List of the Constitution has faced serious problems of responsibility and control because of the apparent conflict among the federal, state and local governments in management of basic education which continually impedes educational development in the country.

Improper Planning

Improper planning usually stems from inaccurate data or statistics on school age population and other educational needs which culminate into poor projections in terms of provision of infrastructure, instructional materials and quality teachers.

Lack of Proper Funding

There is inadequate funding by governments (at federal, state and local levels) as statistics show that federal government expenditure on education has been less than 15 percent of overall expenditure (the highest allocation was 13 percent in 2008) as compared to the UNESCO recommendation of 26 percent of national budget. Also, the menace of corruption is compounding the financing deficit in the implementation of the Universal Basic Education (UBE) programme.

School Drop-Out Rate

The rate of school drop-out depicts the level of access to education by the children. Many reasons, such as the attitude of some parents engaging their children in economic activities, have been adduced as responsible for the increase in the rate of drop-out. This results from lack of confidence in the educational outcome due to poor quality delivery as well as economic conditions of some parents.

Poor Monitoring and Evaluation

This affects the effectiveness of school management and performance of teachers in quality delivery of education under the UBE programme.

Low Level Participation of Stakeholders

The community and the organised private sector appear to have minimal role in UBE programme in spite of their significance in the society. Improvement in public enlightenment will foster greater participation of all stakeholders in the programme.

Poor Motivation of Teachers

The poor condition of teaching staff at primary and secondary education levels aggravates instability in the profession with dare consequences on educational development. Teachers are always prospecting and changing jobs for better remuneration. The lack of stability leads to lack of competent teachers resulting in low teacher-student ratio in the UBE programme, which adversely affects learning outcomes.

Poor Curriculum Delivery

This can only be effective if teachers are trained and equipped with the skills to implement the intended curriculum. Many teachers have no training in teaching with serious consequences on lesson planning and delivery.

Politicisation of Education

Education institutions are set up and run by many state governments based on political considerations rather than achieving goals of education. The negative influence of politicians in the recruitment exercise of teachers is a major constraint in the development of education, particularly at the primary and secondary levels. People without prerequisite knowledge, qualification and training as teachers are recruited to teach in primary and secondary schools, thus destroying the foundation of education.

Indiscipline or Fraud

This manifests in examination malpractices, secret cult menace and corruption. Students are more interested in passing examinations by means other than academic excellence. Regrettably, even parents often encourage this unhealthy behaviour by paying money to agents to ensure that their wards pass the SSCE/NECO/JAMB examinations. The problem of indiscipline is also apparent in the attitude of highly placed staff of these bodies.

Tertiary Education

In Nigeria, education at the tertiary level is mainly divided into the university sector and non-university sector. While the components of the university sector remain the universities themselves, the components of non-university sector are the polytechnics, monotechnics and colleges of education and the specialised institutions. The secondary schools supply the tertiary education sector with students. As at 2013, there were 129 universities, 74 polytechnics, 36 monotechnics and 121 colleges of education. These institutions were both government (federal and states) and privately owned. The significance of tertiary education in the economic growth and development is well embedded in research and advancement in science and technological development which provide solution to diseases, poverty and low productivity. Science and technology are generally seen as instruments for accelerating economic growth through the promotion of creativity and innovation towards redressing issues of poverty and low productivity.

Higher institutions of learning need to ensure that the quality of education they offer meets the expectations of students and the requirements of employers, both today and for the future. Quality of higher education is the responsibility of all stakeholders: government, parents and students, community and employers. The Nigerian government regulatory bodies responsible for the external quality assurance activities at the tertiary education sector are the National Universities Commission (NUC), National Board for Technical Education (NBTE) and National Commission for Colleges of Education (NCCE), which regulate and oversee quality assurance in universities, polytechnics and colleges of education, respectively.

Quality teaching is the use of pedagogical techniques to produce learning outcomes for students. It entails several factors such as effective design of curriculum and course content, a variety of learning contexts (including guided independent study), project-based learning, collaborative learning and experimentation, soliciting and using feedback, and effective assessment of learning outcomes. Importantly, well-adapted learning environments and student support services are necessary components of quality teaching.

The higher education is facing a serious challenge of quality delivery largely due to the enormous pressure from various directions, including inadequate funding, poor teaching and learning facilities, overworked academic staff, incessant academic staff strikes and cultism among students. While quality teaching in tertiary education matters for student learning outcomes, fostering quality teaching remains a major concern to higher education institutions.

The thrust of tertiary education, especially university education, is in advancing knowledge and experience acquired in the process of research and innovation activities. Therefore, tertiary education is expected to prepare students for employment after graduation and equip them with appropriate knowledge, skills, values and attributes to thrive on it. A key issue for institutional leaders and academics is to ensure the balance in fulfilling their teaching and research missions and how to raise the quality of teaching and learning they deliver, whereas the size of an institution is irrelevant with respect to quality teaching. Other issues include the need to strengthen links between teaching and research, among others, by engaging undergraduates in carrying out research as part of the teaching and learning approach.

The cost of higher education around the world has increased tremendously over the years and has even overstretched government budgetary sources. Accordingly, funding of higher education in Nigeria has not met the desired objectives; rather, it generates negative impact on access and quality of higher education. Funding is required for improved access and quality, especially in equipping the schools, hiring quality teachers and providing the necessary services. The combined carrying capacity of tertiary institutions in Nigeria is far from meeting the huge annual applications for admission largely due to lack of adequate physical facilities for teaching and learning. According to the Federal Ministry of Education, the annual applications for admission into the Nigerian tertiary institution are over 1.5 million while the carrying capacity is about 400,000 (FME Annual Report, 2012). In the university system, for example, the NUC introduced a carrying capacity policy which provides that students are admitted based on the facilities available in each university. This policy puts enormous pressure on university admission system in spite of the increase in the number of universities in the country. Whereas the number of secondary school grandaunts has geometrically increased, the space available in universities rather increased arithmetically. Table 31 shows the trend in the university admission system in the last 14 years which indicates that less than 30 percent of the applicants got admissions over the period.

Table 3.1: Total number of universities, applications and admission 1999- 2013

Year	Number of Universities	Number of Applications	Number Admitted	Number left Over
1999/2000	45	417,773	78,550	339,223
2000/2001	46	467,490	50,277	417,213
2001/2002	52	550,399	60,718	544,321
2002/2003	53	994,380	51,845	942,535
2003/2004	54	1,046,950	105,157	941,793
2004/2005	56	841,878	122,492	719,386
2005/2006	75	916,371	N/A	N/A
2006/2007	76	803,472	123,626	679,846
2007/2008	94	1,054,053	194,521	859,532
2008/2009	95	1,182,381	153,000	1,029,381
2009/2010		1,305326	185,209	1,120,117
2010/2011		1,478,258	323,527	1,154,731
2011/2012		1,618,152	331,206	1,286,946
2012/2013		1,628,986	218,324 (ongoing)	1,410,662 (ongoing)

Source: From 2010/2011 the figures are for UTME (formerly UME) used for both university and polytechnic admissions

http://www.ume.com.ng FME 2012 Annual Report.

The ripple effect of the NUC admission policy includes the menace of examination malpractices, whereby students employ unethical means to ensure they pass the UTME examination and the post-UTME screening conducted by universities. This has had serious consequences on the quality of education because many candidates with fake results get their way into universities at the detriment of those with genuine UTME results. Most often, those with fake results do not cope with the academic rigours of undergraduate studies and many withdraw before graduation or manage to graduate with a third class degree status.

Polytechnics, colleges of education and other higher institutions of learning also face funding problems which continually pose a major challenge to the realisation of their potentials in contributing to the growth and development of Nigeria. Lack of adequate funding limits the required infra-structural development in these institutions and generally affects welfare services to staff and students.

In Nigeria, the impact of incessant academic staff strikes on learning outcome of students and, of course, quality of higher education, is very obvious because the strikes have continually paralysed public tertiary education with serious negative effects on the delivery of quality education. Whereas during strikes, students in public tertiary institutions stay out of school, those in private institutions or even abroad are in session. This ugly situation puts unnecessary hardship on most students in Nigeria who spend longer periods in school.

Quality of Education in Economic Development

Nigeria is aiming to become the 20th largest economy by 2020, which no doubt requires her to have increased productivity in manpower with capabilities in abstract and problem-solving skills to tackle the increasingly technological environment of production and services. For Nigeria to compete in the global arena, she requires highly qualified and trained people to perform top-quality research, formulate policies and implement programmes essential to economic growth and development (World Bank, 1989). Central to the goals of universal basic education as encapsulated in the Education for All (EFA) initiative and the Millennium Development Goals targets on education is raising the quality of education for productive human capital towards accelerated economic growth.

Raising the quality of education is dependent on several factors. Most often, in determining the quality of education, important factors like country or area differences are ignored, although one year schooling in India is different from one year schooling in Japan or Sweden. Despite this, research in the economics of growth focuses more on school attainment with no consideration of quality differences or of other sources of learning such as the contribution of families, peers and others. Beyond what happens inside classrooms, educational performance is influenced by other non-school factors.

The importance of cognitive skills – the measure of educational quality – is in its use in determining individual earnings and, by implication, important aspects of the income distribution. This was accentuated by the World Bank (1989), which stated that "empowering people, especially the poor, with basic cognitive skills is the surest way to render them self-reliant citizens". Whereas it is strongly believed that educational attainment has direct effects on earnings and growth, there are other causes for growth. According to Hanushek and Wößmann, overall economic institutions are preconditions to economic development while lack of them may posit a serious constraint to the required impact of education and skills on economic outcomes.

Globalisation has brought about interconnectivity among nations which makes people, capital, information and goods to flow across borders at ever-increasing rates. Consequently, there has been a continuous flow of talent from developing to the developed nations due largely to rapid migration of skilled young people to provide much needed talent in the face of aging workforce in Europe and North America. It is expected that the skills and talents of youth in the developing countries will be the engine of the world's future growth and prosperity. This talent potential can only benefit a developing country where it provides young people with quality education. As the governments in most developing countries are far from providing the needed quantity and quality of education mainly because of competing demands on their scarce resources, it is time for the other beneficiaries of education, especially the private sector, to intervene in the provision of education. Therefore, Nigeria should leverage on her bourgeoning private sector to participate in a more systematic way to funding education. Since the provision of education is a shared responsibility, it is time to act with new energy to invest in providing quality education at all educational levels in the country.

Funding Education

Funding is at the heart of educational management which is a critical aspect that can make or mar the survival of institutions. Lack of proper funding may constrain the growth of any educational institution, especially at higher learning level because of diverse financial needs. The public universities owned by states and federal governments predominate the university system in Nigeria and are mainly funded by the governments. Whereas the federal universities are tuition free, the state universities charge moderate fees compared to private universities which charge tuition fees for their sustenance and to meet their profit motive. Almost all polytechnics and colleges of education are government owned and are also funded through budgetary allocations. The government budgetary sources have been overstretched by other competing societal needs such as health, security, roads and bridges, housing and agriculture. The implications of poor funding have had serious consequences on the education sector. These include the continuous falling standards and quality of education, lack of adequate educational facilities, dilapidation of existing infrastructure and low morale of teachers and lecturers. The budgetary sources also have been hamstrung by non-release of the approved budgets for education. It should be noted that issues of funding of university education is always avoided by stakeholders although the potential solution would be highly beneficial to everyone.

The challenge is to evolve a better means for proper financing of education from the primary to the tertiary level. Sustainable system of funding education is a *sine qua non* to educational development in Nigeria. Therefore, government needs to examine the current funding system with a view to modifying it to meet the present-day requirements. The options may include shared funding system which could foster growth of tertiary education by bringing other stakeholders to intervene in the provision of quality tertiary education in the country. Undergraduate tuition fees may be introduced in the Nigerian universities and other tertiary institutions. It is obvious from the trends in the private education sector, right from the primary to the tertiary education levels, that many parents could afford moderate tuitions fees for their children. However, state and local governments should be encouraged to develop bursaries and education loan schemes with banks for those in need. Government bursaries should to be targeted at those in need, particularly products of public-owned secondary schools while those from the private education sector may rely more on their families. The loan scheme should be structured in a way that beneficiaries would pay back over a period of time on securing employment. Moreso, universities and other institutions of higher learning should harness public-private partnership to attract funding for capital projects and research activities. The introduction of the payment of Education Tax by corporate entities in 1995 has opened a veritable window for funding educational development projects in public-owned institutions through the Tertiary Education Trust Fund (TETFund). Other external sources of funds to compliment the government budgetary allocations should be explored. These include alumni associations, endowments, income from investments and other donor sources.

Primary and secondary education should be supported by corporate bodies and communities with the aim of achieving a more literate society and, more significantly, by fostering creativity and innovation through greater involvement in science and technology to ensure higher economic growth. Because science and technology are major sources for social and economic changes in the history of mankind, as accentuated by Ale, they have "helped to promote health over diseases, food over famine, affluence over poverty, reason over superstition and education over ignorance". Accordingly, it stands to reason that education is a catalyst for progress or economic growth and development. Education, as bedrock for economic growth, requires adequate funding for improved quality which results from appropriately equipping the schools, hiring quality teachers and providing commensurate remuneration.

Mapping the Way Forward

How can governments at all levels and the stakeholders work together to educate the millions of children not in school, build the needed classrooms, and provide and train the necessary teachers. Nigeria's educational development since indepen-dence in 1960 offers insights for the future. Although access to all levels of education has improved significantly, there are still challenges that would require different strategies to make the interaction of education and economic growth mutually beneficial for accelerated development. For example, with increased access to education, the challenge for completion rates remains the problem, especially at junior and senior secondary school levels. The low completion rates deprive the country of the much-needed educated youth prepared for work and for further education and training. To counteract the unprecedented school drop-out syndrome, especially in the rural areas, there is the need for more innovative strategies, including initiatives and incentives that can motivate demand from poorer segments of the country.

Teacher supply and motivation is at the heart of challenge in the quality of education. Hence, in order to stimulate interest in teaching and improving capacity in rural areas, it is important to introduce special incentives for teachers in rural schools such as the provision of special cash allowances and also good housing with pipe-borne water and electricity. Unless this is done, the large majority of children living in rural areas will continue to receive poor quality education. It is significant to develop a well-trained and motivated teaching force to ensure the provision of quality education. Teachers need to enjoy salaries comparable to people with similar qualifications in other professions, if not better. The entry point for teachers needs to be raised to at least Grade Level 09 instead of the current Grade Level 08. In terms of management of resources, the principles of service excellence through enthronement of transparency and accountability in educational management will really foster delivery of quality education at all levels.

The current shortfall in the supply of teachers in primary and secondary schools could be partially addressed by effective utilisation of fresh graduates from tertiary institutions on National Youth Service Corp (NYSC) scheme. At least, in the next six consecutive years, the NYSC programme should concentrate its youth corps workforce to providing services in the education sector. Perhaps, with the exception of medical and health care-related graduates, all NYSC members should be deployed to teach in secondary schools (junior and senior). The six-year period shall serve as a pilot programme, the impact of which could be evaluated on the performance of students over a complete six years of secondary education (junior and senior). This policy will encourage quality graduates to develop interest in teaching services towards enhanced quality education in the country. It may also improve the dignity of the teaching profession in the country. In addition, government should introduce an accelerated teacher development scheme that will, through a structured and special conversion training programme, provide teacher training for non-education graduates for at least a year. Such training will strengthen the ability of would-be teachers to teach in secondary schools which will no doubt increase the quality of teaching in Nigeria.

The challenge for lack of carrying capacity in the tertiary institutions can be partly ameliorated by the use of technology or online resources in teaching and learning. In addition of expanding the Open Distance Learning programme of the National Open University of Nigeria (NOUN), the tertiary institutions need to embrace online resources aimed at greater delivery of education to the populace, and where such initiative is available, it needs to be strengthened. Moreso, the regular courses should combine physical and online teaching so that students may be stationed at different locations but participating in the same class or course. The newly introduced Nigerian Universities Electronic Teaching and Learning Platform in the university system needs to be developed and made available to tertiary education system generally. It will help to overcome the challenge of large classes, foster modern methods of teaching and learning, and content development using interactive tools.

In financing terms, the challenge for educational planners and administrators is about how best balanced growth in education can be achieved within realistic budget constraints with appropriate shares for primary, secondary and tertiary education, more significantly, how best they can mobilise funding from the community and the private sector to complement the government budgetary sources. Proper funding of education will enable the financing of acquisition of necessary facilities and expanded student enrolment, as well as employment of teachers who will be highly motivated, conscientious and efficient. This will no doubt foster the production of quality human resources accelerated growth and development of the country.

Conclusion

In order to achieve greater quality of education in Nigeria, it is imperative that the governments at all levels should consider a radical transformation in the mechanism of quality control and quality assurance which remain the foundation for the realisation of quality education. Realising access to quality education requires that governments (federal, state and local), community leaders, developers, planners and educators, as well as the organised private sector or employers work together to plan and develop education. They should leverage on diverse resources, including innovative partnerships that weave together diverse funding sources to maximise resources for education. It is safe to conclude that education alone will not be the ultimate solution to the elusive quest for growth, as there are other factors such as appropriate structural economic reforms which create incentives to improve economic efficiency, increase investment and adopt new technologies.

4

Feeding the Future: Agriculture in the New World Order

O n the 27-kilometre stretch between Ologbo and Koko in the Warri North Local Government Area of Delta State, lies a vast and expansive palm plantation which occupies about a fifth of that road space. It is called the "COWAN Estate" and dates back to the 1960s when competing public sector-managed commercial plantations thrived in the regions of the country.

On the other side of the old Bendel State, precisely in Urhonigbe, lies the Nigerian Institute for Oil Palm Research (NIFOR) and another expansive plantation to which was added the famous research centre which the Malaysians came to collect seedlings with which to commence their own palm oil industry. Today, that South East Asian nation has the distinction of being the leading player in palm oil cultivation and processing worldwide, even as Nigeria has since sadly receded into a net importer of the product.

The case for a comprehensive overhaul of the agricultural sector in Nigeria today, however, goes beyond lamenting with nostalgia over treasures lost. It is about a more pragmatic need to recognise the critical imperative of this age-old foundational sector and then proceed to interrogate how maximally we can benefit from it. This is because, while it is true that in the past, the plantations provided ample job opportunities for many Nigerians, it is also to be noted that our agricultural sector was, even then, not just a plantation-based one. It was a robust arena that had long satisfied the first reason for the emergence and development of the craft, namely, food security. Indeed, it is to be noted that the primary reason why our agriculture deficit is so obvious today is that we are really now not in a position to grow and cultivate enough of our preferred staple crops to feed all of our people at affordable costs.

Between Agriculture and Employment

There is also the corollary of the relationship between the agricultural enterprise and provision of jobs for citizens, and going beyond that to the availability of gainful and competitive employment in the sector. As data on the importance of agriculture as a job creation mechanism reveals, about one-third of all the workers in the world are today engaged in agriculture. Here in Nigeria, as is the case in many developing countries, the figures are astounding with the sector providing employment for three-quarters of the engaged workforce in the country. Indeed, if Chinua Achebe had described the Nigerian crisis, in *The Trouble with Nigeria*, as "simply and squarely a failure of leadership", we can draw a parallel and say that given the sheer mass of our people that are engaged in the agricultural sector today, the nation's crisis of poverty, unemployment and under-employment very heavily rests on our gross inability to grow the sector in such a way that it would be maximally efficient and prosperous, and guarantee food security for the nation, profits for entrepreneurs and living wages for employees. So, getting it right with the agricultural sector in Nigeria is critically important for many reasons.

Food Security, Human Dignity, Peace and National Stability

In William Shakespeare's very compelling play, *As You Like It*, the story is told of how after enduring days of hunger, deprivation and the near death of his servant and benefactor, Adam, the erstwhile gentle and well-cultured son of Sir Rowland de Boys, Orlando, had, on seeing the family of the banished Duke of one of the provinces of France about to sit down and eat in the forests of Arden, literally lost his cool. He pulled out his sword and threatened: "Eat no more; I must have your food!" It is sad but true: the absence of food does make monsters of the gentlest of men. And the opposite gender does not indeed fare much better. Across Nigeria today, the number of young ladies and sometimes married women who are pushed into compromising situations on account of the need to just get a meal or a ticket to continuous feeding for themselves and sometimes too, their loved ones also, is rather alarming. Indeed, we dare hypothesise that one primary way to begin to restore the moral foundations of the Nigerian state today is to ensure that there is decent and affordable provision of food for all her citizens.

Indeed, food is a very basic and most critical human need. Once in every few hours, every normal human being feels the pangs of hunger and the need for food. When this need is not satiated, it leads to loss of focus, reduced productivity and lower mental alertness. Providing food for people, therefore, is imperative in the country's march towards a progressive society. A government that invests in the provision of food for its people is one that guarantees security and stability. It is that basic.

Indeed, taking the discourse beyond the prism of food as a basic human need, one would be confronted with the fact that history is peppered with examples which confirm that a country that cannot provide food for her citizens is a sure bet for disaster. And so, from Carthage to Sparta, Trier to Constantinople, a food and provisions blockade was one of the prized regular weapons that well-heeled generals, through antiquity, quickly deployed to gain the advantage in the course of the prosecution of their very many wars and battles.

Even more recently, and as was evidenced in the crisis in the defunct Soviet Union, the fact that in many of the years of the Cold War era, that behemoth of a nation could almost not provide enough food for her citizens was indeed a fundamental blight on her overall fighting capacity. Currently, the inability of the communist regime in North Korea to adequately meet the food needs of its population has continued to be an annoying albatross and a check (but significantly quite providential benefit for many of the other peace-loving peoples of the world) to its propensity and desire to damn its southern neighbour, and beyond them, "the west and the rest of us".

Second, there is the issue of costs and affordability. In a number of nations where food prices have risen to astronomic levels, the governments of those nations have seen their continuing capacity to rule very sorely taxed. The French Revolution is one such example when a spike in the cost of bread led to a lot of untoward circumstances. There was widespread rioting in the streets and the execution, via the guillotine, of the bumbling Emperor, Louis, and the infamous Queen, Antoinette, of the "if-the-people-cannot-find-bread-then-give-them-cake" fame. There was also the wholesale overthrow of the old monarchical order and its subsequent replacement with the current republican system of government. More recently, there have been even more examples ranging from Sudan to the Philippines, Algeria, Egypt and Tunisia, where skyrocketting food prices have been a principal catalyst in the shaking up, or even outright removal, of governments.

Imperative of Creative and Comprehensive Solutions

In looking for solutions to Nigeria's current agriculture crisis then, it is important to be as comprehensive as possible. Accordingly, we would spare no effort in going down memory lane as far as we must, even as we commit to essentially thinking out of the box. In this wise, one very first thing to disabuse our minds of is the penchant to discriminate between indigenous food types and foreign or imported varieties. If truth be told, making this distinction is really quite difficult. This is because while some crops like wheat are today considered essentially non-indigenous, the reality is that there was also a time when some of our otherwise older crop types were also blatantly foreign. For example, it took the coming of the Portuguese in the 16th century to introduce maize and cassava into large swathes of the African continent. This "new foreign crop", within a very short time, went on to replace some of the erstwhile dominant and traditional African crops and grew to become two of "the continent's most important staple food crops" for very many years.

Another notable argument that deflates this insistence on consuming only indigenously produced food borders on the pragmatic. As studies have demonstrated, three cereals, namely, rice, corn and wheat, provide 60 percent of human food supply today. Why change a winning team? And does this seriously underperforming developing country have the resources, political will and enforcement capacity to literally "kick against the goads" as some of our "only-the-indigenous" proponents would have us do? On the platform of our scale of preference as a nation, is this the most critical battle to take on now? Do basic existence and continuing survival not yet precede essence?

Related to this is the basic error inherent in the position of the ordinarily well-meaning environmental activists who have now made a religion of sorts out of their outright rejection of hybrid crop and food varieties, whereas the evidence on the ground and indeed through history, counsel otherwise. Yes, agri-business may sometimes go to the extreme. Yes, there is the need to be circumspect about the potentially unsavoury health implications of a regime of genetically modified foods. But then we also must not just throw away the baby with the bath water. This is because, given the scope of the food crisis that the world is confronted with today, one core task that must remain uppermost in our minds is how to feed our teeming population at affordable costs. In this challenge, we can benefit from both ancient history and modern science. If primitive observation gave us some of the initial food varieties that we still subsist on, advanced and contemporary scientific methods will surely come in handy in resolving the grave food challenges that this generation of God's divine creation is faced with.

Overview of the Nigerian Agricultural Sector

A study carried out in 1990 identified 82 million hectares out of Nigeria's total land area of about 91 million hectares to be arable. However, only 42 percent of this total cultivable area was then being farmed, which meant that much unlike many of the nations of the world which have sparse cultivable land areas but which still go ahead to record huge agricultural yields on account of their introduction of time and cost efficient management and technological processes into the sector, the Nigerian agricultural sector was still under-performing even in ordinary terms.

Today, the continuing march of urbanisation and environmental degradation has combined to reduce the volume of cultivable land to about 80 million hectares. But even that is still more than enough to make the nation an agricultural power if we get our sectoral basics right and make the critical inputs and reforms that the industry has been begging for throughout the decades since Independence.

A second deficit had to do with the fact that much of the land being farmed at this time was done under the clearly inefficient bush fallow system, whereby the land is left idle for a period of time after its use to allow for the natural regeneration of soil fertility.

Equally, of the overall cultivable national land stock, 18 million hectares were classified as permanent pasture. But it is clear that with better and cooperative management methods, even these pasture lands still have the potential to support crops. Further, a sizeable component of the remaining stock, which came up to as much as 20 million hectares at the time of the study, was covered by forests and woodlands. On this also, agronomists expressed their belief that, with improved management methods, a sizeable chunk of these lands equally possessed quite impressive agricultural potential.

As for the directly cultivated mass, it yet suffers from a myriad of challenges and difficulties leading to a scenario where the country continued to suffer in the midst of plenty. First, there was the prevalence of a system in which agricultural holdings were not only small and scattered, but their actual cultivation was also carried out with very simple and rudimentary tools. Large-scale agriculture was not common and indeed almost lacking. Notwithstanding this disadvantage, the sector was still able to contribute large swathes of the nation's GDP. How much of this has changed as we write?

If we look at official statistics which reveal that agriculture contributed 32 percent of the nation's GDP as at 2011, we may very well miss the point. This is because this fairly impressive figure, rather than being a specific measure of how well we have grown and developed agriculture in Nigeria, points more to the equally troubling overall lack of capacity utilisation and real growth in other sectors of the economy, and very notably, the petroleum sector which commentators have variously labelled as "the curse of oil" or "the Dutch disease".

However, the reality remains that the nation's agricultural sector, if properly developed, can contribute far greater volume in real-time employment capacity, value creation and, of course, GDP and GNP terms. The challenge then is to get into the "proper development mode".

In achieving this, it is our view that there are three critical elements around which our national agricultural development strategy should be built. The first is food for domestic consumption. The second is production for export. And the third has to do with agro-processing and the integration of agriculture and agricultural products into other industrial sectors. This distinction made, let us now go into greater detail, element by element.

Domestic Food Production

Today, the bulk of Nigeria's agricultural production fits into this category. While this is most commendable, the fact that the nation is still a net importer of food despite the large number of her citizens not yet engaged in producing food for domestic consumption immediately points to the presence of certain "errors in rendering" within this sector. Let us look at them in terms of the time-tested "factors of production", the first of which is land.

The Land Crisis

Two difficulties immediately confront us when we look at the issue of land and its contribution to our low domestic food output. The first has to do with the historical process of traditional family land inheritance where at the demise of the patriarch, the extant stock of land in the family holdings is shared among "surviving" family members. With averagely very large family sizes and ever increasing population figures to boot, the overall quantum of land available to individuals for farming purposes has, therefore, continued to shrink.

The second difficulty has to do with the continued retention in our statutes of the very crippling and growth-defeating Land Use Act, 1978. In vesting the ultimate ownership of all land stock existing within the country in the hands of the state, the law introduces significant and very practical cost and process difficulties for the small-scale "farmer" (and well over 98 percent of our existing farming population belong here) who wishes to acquire land for essentially agricultural purposes. This is particularly compounded by the fact that this subsistence farmer is in competition with other better endowed "cash crop farmers" and other more robust sectors – as the real estate industry, for example – for the very scarce allocation paper or "C of O".

For agriculture, being a land-based vocation, the continued retention of the land use act in its present form and shape is one of the biggest hindrances to the development of the sector in Nigeria. This is because by continuing to insist that land, which is the first capital element for the farmer, does not really belong to him except and until he can persuade the Governor of his state to confirm so and be ready to pay the huge rents that government has imposed on this vital stock. The state has virtually "muzzled the ox that treads the grain". And the scripture is very clear in its insistence that this would not bring about a blessing for those involved in the obnoxious practice.

To get around these difficulties, it is recommended that the President of the Federal Republic of Nigeria should bring in the weight of his office to drive a consensual plan that will see to the complete review of the Land Use Act. We will get to other solutions subsequently.

Capital makes the Difference

As a banker, it is a well-known fact that financing does indeed play a crucial role in the translation of dreams to reality. Of course, it is not everything, but its absence does indeed have huge implications for the possibility of dreams succeeding. In our context here, it is critical that we find a way to ensure that our food producers can find capital with which to pursue their bankable proposals.

This capital intervention would begin with their tutoring in elementary finance, bookkeeping, financial literacy, business structure and the imperative of ensuring that they cultivate the right discipline and integrity regimen without which success and sustainable progress would not be achieved.

To these should then be added a large pool of funds that would be jointly guaranteed by government and the banking sector which would be disbursed to bankable proposals along with firmly built-in agricultural extension and project monitoring processes that would help ensure the maximum efficiency of this intervention package.

"Help! There is no Labour Here Anymore!"

It may sound alarmist but it is true! By the day, the continuing stock of available labour to work the farms and produce the food we crave to find on our tables daily has been vastly depleted. Urbanisation is one omnibus villain and this can yet be tackled by a conscious programme to provide the good things of life (potable water, decent housing, roads, electricity, telephone and Internet access, recreational facilities, etc) in and around our farming communities, as well as a conscious programme to raise the standard of living of farm workers. As we are writing this, a lot of young people in rural farming communities who have been long weaned on a diet of poverty, lack and deprivation, continue to lust for "the break" that will take them out: just give me something, anything in the city and I will go – porter! security guard! cook! driver! cleaner! commercial motorbike rider! Just anything! Yes, our urban centres need the blue collar workers but should not be at the expense of the food production that we all need and must get, daily!

But then there is another devil and it has to do with the relative lack of contemporary skill and value in the peasant culture that many of our farm communities remain trapped in. Given the levels of advancement in the world today, the average human being has come to be motivated to believe that his life must count for something! What education and skills acquisition do for us in this respect is basically fundamental: it gives us "a place to stand from where we can go on to then move the world!"

Confronted with the near-absence of anything valuable within the peasant farming milieu that would answer this pang in their heart, many a young person that is very much needed in our farms soon switches career, aspiration and direction. And so we continue to have unfulfilled citizens, a hungry nation and little real growth, overall.

For agriculture to be meaningful today, we must transit to a new regime of large and well-funded mechanised farms that pay living wages and provide sufficient catalysts for self-actualisation. Our farming population must be able to see that their profession is as noble as any other and that farming is indeed good, literally!

Wanted: Domestic Food Entrepreneurs

As they say, we have kept the best for the last. Enterprise involves training, no doubt. But it also has to do very significantly with mindset. This is why, for example, all through history, some of the most potent and astounding success examples have been of ordinary people who rose from obscurity, defied all odds, fought the waves and made a mark where they had been written off. If we take the example of the modern state of Israel, we find here an example of a state that continues to brave many odds to barely exist. And in so doing, it has been able to achieve significant traction to excel in many areas and respects.

Returning to our subject, it is apparent to me that at the heart of our domestic food production incapacities may very well be the absence of a system-impacting entrepreneurial spirit amidst the core of our extant food producers.

With a disposition to soar beyond the skies and not take no for an answer, these *food-preneurs* would then go on to find solutions to the earlier identified hurdles and more.

With firm attention to resolving these limitations, we would then be able to get back to our pre-civil war era when the country was self-sufficient in domestic food production and even go further to our land of domestic food abundance.

Today, other than bread which is largely produced out of imported American wheat, some of the most demanded food crops are yams and cassava in the south and sorghum and millet in the north. With the reforms we have suggested here, it would only be a matter of time before our present domestic food production handicaps would be overcome.

Cash Crop Farming, Agro-Processing and Agro- Business

Existentialists argue that existence precedes essence, meaning that you must live before you can add value to life and indeed, anything else. This is why we first addressed the issue of domestic food production because only a well-fed people can go on to attain higher levels of progress.

Having disposed of that preliminary need, let us now go on to issues that border on wealth creation, employment generation, dignity enhancement and greater overall fulfilment in the agriculture enterprise.

For centuries now, humanity has come to accept the fact that one of the ways to get the agricultural produce or derivatives of it that you need but which your climate and topography do not permit you to cultivate is to get it from elsewhere. This applies to food crops and also in the arena of cash crop cultivation and agro-processing.

Indeed, historians would tell you that this imperative of producing crops for more than individual or family subsistence is at the heart of the systems of human development that we have seen after the first epoch of the early man who was essentially a hunter and gatherer of chance foodstuff. The development of clans, villages and towns followed hard upon this logic. Slaves were needed because of this and even the entire colonisation process had the cultivation of more and more crops for the metropolitan economy as an undisguised *raison d'être*.

Here in Nigeria in particular, the development of the plantations and the cash crop economy that literally sustained the nation in the emergent era of European-denominated modernisation followed along this pattern all through the era of colonial rule and after it, in the immediate post-colonial era. In the South West of the country, cocoa was the leading cash crop for very many years until dependence on oil as the nation's pre-eminent foreign exchange earner. The dominance of smallholders and lack of farm labour due to urbanisation led to gross production declines. In 1999, for example, Nigeria produced just about 145,000 tons of cocoa beans even when it had the potential for over 300,000 tons.

A second cash crop, rubber, which may still be the second largest non-oil foreign exchange earner, was popularised within the colonial era and extensively grown in plantations within the South South and South East regions of Nigeria.

We have also talked about oil palm which was equally cultivated in the southern belt of Nigeria and which for many years was indeed a net foreign exchange earner. Indeed, the records do attest to the fact that not only was palm oil from Nigeria a net cash crop and foreign exchange earner, much of the initial contact and trade between Nigeria and Europe was predicated upon the acknowledgement by the extant European powers that the area surrounding the famous River Niger, and most notably, the Bight of Benin and Bight of Biafra areas, were an inexhaustible source of palm produce that fed the soap and associated body care industries of Manchester and other developing industrial centres in the West. To underscore this point is the fact that when the early explorers, colonial cartographers and government bureaucrats looked for a fitting name for the area from which they derived this immense wealth, they quickly agreed on one: The Oil Rivers Protectorate.

Again, it is the economic importance and significance of this "red gold" area even then that also had the paradoxical effect of excessive British interest in subduing the dominant political systems in the area and replacing them with a more pliant "indirect rule" varieties. From Bonny to Ebrohimi, Akassa to Opobo, Brass, Old Calabar and Benin, the British colonialists ensured that leaders like King Jaja, Nanna Olomu and Ovonramwen Nogbaisi were all forcibly dethroned.

Independence and the Cash Crop Economy

The advent of full and formal Independence in October, 1960, was preceded by a period of limited self rule. During this period, the indigenous premiers of the respective regions built on the cash crop economic base of their regions. In the West, Chief Obafemi Awolowo led an administration that continued to generate the bulk of its revenues from cocoa, palm produce and rubber. In the South East, rubber and palm produce were strong economic contributors that the Nnamdi Azikiwe/Michael Okpara governments built on while Sir Ahmadu Bello led a Northern Region whose core revenues came from the groundnut pyramids of Kano.

More Recommendations for Growing the Nigerian Agricultural Sector

Mechanisation/Industrialisation

One of the critical challenges in growing the agricultural sector in Nigeria has to do with the issue of the lack of mechanisation of the sector. As a component of industrialisation, the mechanisation of the agricultural sector has brought in a lot of benefits for beneficiary communities. In Europe and North America, for example, mechanisation encouraged the reduction in the number of people physically engaged in agriculture even with productivity levels being boosted. Other benefits of mechanisation include food processing, improved storage facilities, greater financial yields and increased crop output.

Food Security and National Greatness

The point has often been made that there is indeed no country that truly becomes great without achieving basic self-sufficiency in food production for her citizens. Take the state of Israel, for example. Given her location and relative state of isolation within the Middle East region, it would have been an unmitigated disaster if it had not been able to proactively develop her agricultural capacities, notwithstanding her very obvious natural, climatic and environmental handicaps, to provide food for both her people and for export. Thus, the Zionist nation is not vulnerable today to food shocks that could have more calamitous consequences than nuclear weapons.

It is equally to be noted that food availability helps to curtail inflationary trends. As at the time of writing, for example, data from the National Bureau of Statistics was pointing to the fact that inflation rates were now hovering at 7.9 percent, a figure clearly more manageable than the double digit scenario of a few years before now. It is this continuing attention by successive administrations to improve conditions for local food production that has helped the nation stave the negatives that showed up during the 2008 global food crisis as well as the global warming induced flooding that affected large swathes of the nation in the second half of 2012.

These strides notwithstanding, it is to be noted that the current strides recorded in our agricultural sector are yet a far cry from the golden era of agricultural production that the nation witnessed in the early years of independence. It is also not good enough for where we should be playing agriculturally today – among the host of nations that feed themselves, export excess produce, have become strongly mechanised, process agricultural produce beyond their primary forms, have very developed food processing infrastructure and whose agro-enterprises are maximally efficient, profitable ongoing concerns and employees well-remunerated.

Until oil grew to become the king revenue earner for the country that it is now, agriculture was our veritable cash cow. There were the groundnut pyramids, the cotton and cocoa plantations, rubber, palm and other cash crops of yesteryears that largely financed the development plans and activities that the nation depended on in those early years. But then the curse of oil came, leading to a massive neglect of agriculture and the results are all so obvious today.

Regression since Independence

At Independence, Nigeria was not only able to feed herself, cash crop farming also provided the mainstay for the economies of the three regions that made up the country. The West had crops like cocoa, palm produce and rubber; the East had palm produce and rubber, and the North had hides and skins, millet, groundnuts and sorghum. Indeed, the famous groundnut pyramids of Kano were sympathetic of the agricultural and economic boom of that era.

In more recent years, however, these preliminary advantages have been eroded leading to a drop in the sector's net contribution to the nation's GDP and indeed her overall viability. Other problems associated with this state of regression include the vast numbers of able-bodied citizens who migrated from villages to the urban centres and the consequent rise in the average age of the Nigerian farmer.

Primary Producers

The high agricultural production levels that were experienced during the Independence era notwithstanding, the nation generally remained at the level of primary producers. This is unacceptable as a focus on primary produce in a world where premium profits come from value addition, is in itself a choice for the back-end of the chain. While primary production is the basic starting point for all agricultural activities, there is a need to go beyond that and move on to bring in integrated secondary and tertiary production activities into the mix. For example, in the cultivation of cocoa, there is the primary planting and harvesting of the cocoa plant. This is later shelled for the pods to be released and then sent for processing. Until lately, a lot of the processing at this level took place outside of the country. Even now that processing takes place in a few centres, it is, however, still at the rudimentary level as it is further exported for even more tertiary processing before it returns in its final processed form to be used as raw material for the production of creams, beverages and the likes. Needless to say that a huge premium has been introduced on the product before it is returned which ultimately translates to higher purchasing costs for the end-user.

Food Types

In Nigeria today, the crisis in the agricultural sector is best exemplified by the huge volume of rice and wheat imports. This is strange because until a few years ago, both crops were conveniently categorised as largely foreign and minority crops with very limited and essentially urban patronage. Over time, however, cultural attitudes shifted to the current situation where both food types have not only grown in their position as star staple foodstuff in the country, they have also become net imports and a substantial drain on the nation's scarce foreign exchange stock.

Recently, there have been efforts to ensure indigenous participation in the production of these and other basic product types. This needs to be aggressively promoted so that the average citizen can get the full benefit of the corrective measures.

Right Steps

The Ministry of Agriculture in Nigeria has, for example, moved to tame the hitherto widespread incidence of corruption in fertilizer sales and allocations. This was a huge problem but it has been reasonably addressed through the recently introduced voucher system that helps to ensure that the commodity does not get mired in the politics of obdurate middlemen and profiteering by influential speculators.

Equally, there have been efforts to ensure that some of the benefits of new technological systems as mobile telephony and the Internet and, in particular, their capacity for enhanced and widespread communication and outreach, do get to farmers, no matter how small or remotely located. Given the centrality of agricultural extension services in boosting and growing new sector, this is one area that we urge governments at various levels to pay serious attention in the future.

Pastoral Farming Reforms

The present situation where cattle rearers trek long distances from the north of Nigeria and beyond, to bring their animals to the markets of the south, is not time and cost effective. Also, their reported brushes with local crop farmers who resent the damage the cattle inflict on crop stock, is also unfortunate. In fact, these clashes have risen to alarming proportions in recent years, often sparking off communal strife and contributing to the increasing spectre of the violence in the country. A win-win situation has to be provided for the two segments of the food industry concerned to cooperate, cohabit and grow in a more inter-related and dynamic framework.

Infrastructure and Food Processing

These are two critical limitations that continue to assail our farming environment. The absence of good quality motorable roads, for example, has led now and again to the maintenance of the very discouraging scenario where farm crops perish and wither away while in transit from rural farming locations to urban markets.

For the agricultural sector to grow beyond its present capacity, government must provide access roads. This should be done at all levels starting with the very critical local government areas that should provide motorable dirt roads, earth roads, bush tracks and other more advanced construction.

Also, modern amenities should be provided to attract and retain the youthful labour force notably with which a lot gets done. In certain situations, the additional infrastructure needs would truly be crop-specific. In the cultivation of rice, for example, threshing and de-stoning mills that individual farmers cannot buy should be centrally purchased, operated and maintained.

Equally important here would be the revival of the culture of school farms and sundry "catch them young" schemes as well as the re-introduction of agricultural practicals in the school curriculum and a culture of knowledgeable orientation talks on the importance and benefits of farming. Just like the Americans rigorously market their armed forces to school-age and school-leaving youths, Nigeria must put in place a creative marketing mechanism to get our young people back to the farms.

Equally, unavailable and inadequate rain harvesting and irrigation infrastructure has resulted in a situation where farmers are subjected to the vagaries of the elements, resulting in lower yields and diminished output.

It would be most important here to address these failings that continue to threaten the nation's food security and adequacy status. Good roads must be built and maintained and more irrigation and rain harvesting projects embarked upon to guarantee critical all-year round water supply that would help the nation transit to a more productive agricultural regime of multiple harvests within the annual cycle.

The development of our food processing complex would also help to solve the huge problem of waste in the sector today. Driving through Benue, Plateau and Nassarawa states, for example, the traveller is confronted with the sceptre of huge fruits and other agricultural produce that are literally falling off the trees and begging to be moved to markets immediately or processed for secondary consumption. At the Mile 12 market in Lagos also, a lot of food gets wasted on account of faulty economics, poor storage, nil processing and the absence of a basic scheme of backward integration that will, for example, see food items left unsold at the close of a trading day, being passed on to a bulk processor whose business it is to convert same into secondary products that would introduce win-win benefits for farmers, marketers, consumers and indeed the nation.

Silos should be more Active

Within the country today, a number of grain reserves and silos have been put in place to receive and store excess food crops that cannot be consumed at the time of harvest. While this is a salutary step in itself, there is the need to increase the volume and quantity of such silos in the country while also expanding the brief of the silo management scheme towards ensuring that it has even greater and more beneficial impact on other critical economic indicators within and beyond the nation's shores. For example, in many of the rice and wheat producing nations of Asia, Europe and North America, there is a deliberate programme to fill up their silos not only to get food that could be distributed within the domestic scene when the need arises but also as a strategic factor of international trade, global competition, foreign policy, foreign exchange management and the raising of the standard of living of the average farmer. For these countries then, food is a buffer. It is also an asset and could yet serve as a means of securing the very critical edge in relation with other nations when the need arises. Fair is fair!

Cooperatives to the Rescue

Sometimes, the difficulty that the average banker has with passing on credit to farmers is the fact that they just do not hit the page in banking terms. The introduction of functional cooperatives in the country would help to address this nagging issue of small and unviable holdings. It would also help in getting better returns on products for farmers, shared costs in mechanisation, marketing, etc. It can also be used as comfort to attract credit with which to grow the income of the individual farmer and indeed the overall farming community.

Research and Development

Contemporary agricultural practice does not just involve putting seeds into the ground and waiting for them to grow. It is an intensive business practice that is heavily fuelled by best practices in research and development. For the Nigerian agricultural sector to be further boosted, it is imperative that this critical segment has to be properly integrated and advanced.

Some of the issues that would benefit the nation from that arena would, for example, be finding solutions to the issue of long-range pastoral grazing, the production of multiple yields within a calendar year and the introduction of disease-resistant seed varieties.

Gardening and Re-Orientation

In the past, empty spaces around homes were often used for gardening. Now, it is chic to cement all the ground around the house. This only allows for ornamental potted plants for those who insist on some green.

Going forward, it would be necessary to commence an enlightenment campaign to get as many of our citizens as possible to re-engage the very helpful past-time of gardening. While this would have immediate benefits of leisure for the younger population, engagement for retirees and savings in the family budget on items now planted in the gardens that ordinarily would have been purchased elsewhere, there is also an opportunity for inculcating in the younger generation, a love for the field that could very well be a critical seed in the raising of the next generation of farmers.

Promotion of Local Agriculture Festivals

To get individuals and communities to develop an even stronger love for farming and agricultural practice, it is important to organise events like agricultural festivals where success and achievement in the fields would be showcased and celebrated. The Argungu Fishing Festival in the North, the New Yam Festivals in the South East, etc, are some such activities that should be encouraged and boosted.

Combating the Challenge of Pollution

As we write today, pollution is vastly depleting the fish stock within the Niger Delta region. For a traditionally aquatic people who built their economy around marine produce, it is important that everything is done to curb the currently very high levels of pollution that are traceable to poor oil mining practices in the region.

Much unlike in the past when fishing was the mainstay of many a resident of the Niger Delta, today the incidence of oil pollution has led to swamps and creeks where almost no fishing takes place, leaving the nation to be a net importer of a commodity that the country is so richly blessed with.

Akinwunmi Adesina is, at the time of writing this book, the Minister of Agriculture in Nigeria. Widely seen as a most determined achiever, the Minister came up with sundry schemes and initiatives to redress the nation's low fortunes in the agricultural arena. And the world has taken notice. Early in 2014, for example, he was named the *Forbes* Magazine Man of the Year. But awards are not everything as the Minister found out in the course of a March 2014 visit to Lagos where he discovered a cold room that was stacked with cartons of rotten fish. Enraged, he ordered the closure of the place and vowed to go after all such centres in the country.

Part of the Minister's pain over the discovery was the fact that it was happening at the time the nation was investing heavily in fish cultivation to ensure that Nigeria returned to her earlier heyday status when she was self-sufficient in fish production.

And in a related outburst on yet another instance of economic sabotage, the Minister recently bemoaned the inability of the Nigeria Customs Service and related security agencies to help check the continued influx of imported rice into the country despite a subsisting ban on rice importation and sundry efforts by government to ensure that the nation produces all of the rice that she needs.

We are in sympathy with the Minister and his initiatives because we are very well aware of the fact that underscoring Nigeria's difficulties in the food arena are the vast sums spent on the importation of food into the country.

Even more problematic is the fact that the nation's taste for foreign food has today assumed the status of near cultural dependency. And the danger in continuing with this aberrant food taste is that it could invariably have a huge dent on the nation's foreign exchange outflow and circumscribe real-time economic growth. The prognosis is indeed not good. And this should not be. Not with the composite data on the nation. In its 2012 report, for example, the World Bank noted that at more than 160 million people, the population of Nigeria is the largest in Africa and accounts for 47 percent of West Africa's total population. Given that a large population like this immediately translates to a large market and a large workforce, two of the critical variables for growth in the world today, then there really should be no reason why the country should be in the dire economic straits in which it is enthralled today. This is moreso when the same nation is also the biggest oil exporter in Africa and indeed one with the continent's largest natural gas reserves.

Indeed, on the positive side, Nigeria's oil wealth has helped to maintain relatively steady economic growth despite recent global financial downturns. Buoyed by these assets, the country's GDP, the Bank documents, grew from 6 percent in 2008 to 8.4 percent in 2010. On the negative side, however, the continuing inability of the nation's political and economic managers to firmly diversify her economic base has resulted in the aberrant situation where unemployment remains a significant problem in the country with an estimated 50 million youth unemployed at the time of writing.

And here indeed is the rub. Agriculture, on account of its inherent capacity to attract large volumes of people in its work-structure clearly remains the easiest way out of the unemployment crisis in the country. What is, therefore, needed is the right complement of strategies and policies that would translate into jobs for these Nigerians.

Recognising this, the Central Bank of Nigeria set up an agricultural fund as part of its contribution to help deepen the sector. While there is little evidence of how well and how far that scheme has been prosecuted, there is still an obviously crying need for the Nigerian state to create a pool of funds that is accessible to farmers and would-be farmers at less than the currently applicable market rate and which will be used to promote local agricultural cultivation and the improvement of the associated value chain. Multilateral support is also encouraged to be sought so that the quantum of funds available for the scheme would indeed be commensurate to the huge task that we have at hand and its massive financing needs which is to ensure basic self-sufficiency in the core agricultural staples that are consumed in the country.

Equally, while we support the large-scale job creation in the agricultural sector, we must, however, emphasise that this must essentially be with a firm commitment to value creation and addition through the use of modern agricultural machinery and agricultural economics. There is no point in the 21st century to simply give our young people crude implements to go and hew endlessly at hard soils that can be cultivated with tractors and other modern machinery even as they busy themselves with the application of the results of high quality research and development schemes in the area of net yields per acreage, improved crop varieties and the resultant net contribution of the agricultural sector to the nation's GDP and, indeed, the overall economy.

Population (1000's) 2010		158,423	
GDP 2011			243,985,812,280 $
GNI Per Capita 2011		1,280 $	
FDI 2011			8,841,952,784 $
Inflation 2011			2.34 %
Consumer Price Index 1990	8.20		

Food Security	
Calorie Supply per Capita 2009	2,711
Population undernourished 2010-12	8.50 %
Under 5 Mortality Rate (per 1,000) 2010	143.00

Agric. Production	*2007*	*2008*	*2009*	*2010*
Rice Production	3,186,000 MT	4,179,000 MT	3,546,250 MT	4,472,520 MT
Wheat Production	44,000 MT	53,000 MT	36,813 MT	34,200 MT
Maize Production	6,724,000 MT	7,525,000 MT	7,358,260 MT	7,676,850 MT
Soybean Production	580,000 MT	591,000 MT	610,000 MT	285,050 MT

Agricultural Exports	*2006*	*2007*	*2008*	*2009*
Rice Exports	2,497 MT	251.00 MT	46.00 MT	1.00 MT
Wheat Exports	15.00 MT	82.00 MT	12.00 MT	12.00 MT
Maize Exports	3,666 MT	10,416 MT	1,023 MT	1,023 MT
Soybean Exports	11,500 MT	15,300 MT	15,000 MT	14,400 MT

Agric. Imports	2005	2006	2007	2008
Rice Imports	1,187,786 MT	975,907 MT	1,216,962 MT	971,815 MT
Wheat Imports	3,714,680 MT	3,244,000 MT	7,795,100 MT	1,132,180 MT
Maize Imports	17,668 MT	9,612 MT	687.00 MT	49.00 MT
Soybean Imports	23,124 MT	23,124 MT	23,124 MT	83.00 MT

Source: Food Portal.

5

ICT and the Challenge of Sustainable Development

A s our exegesis continues, we realise that Nigeria today is afflicted by a wide gamut of developmental challenges: education, skills development, capacity building, employment and nation building. There is clear admission that a lot needs to be done. In all of these, however, there is about no other sector known to man today that could literally catapult a people's fortune as information and communication technology (ICT). Across the world, today's leading nations are those at the forefront of the deployment of effective and revolutionary ICT solutions in solving age-old and complex problems. And even on the level of individual and personal achievement, many of the individual success stories in the world today (with one or more notable exceptions) are essentially ICT-exploring entrepreneurs. Nigeria, therefore, can only win with a well-developed and firmly-enhanced ICT sector. And we are definitely not alone in this conclusion.

Chrisanthi Angerou, in the article titled, "Discourses on Innovation and Development in Information Systems in Developing Countries", outlines the point that in general techno-economic thought, there is overwhelming consensus that the lifeblood that transmits the needed vital force for the realisation of durable, qualitative and quantitative growth and real development in any economy, are the twin engines of knowledge and information, and how they are deployed.

Of these, ICT - an embodiment of multi-complex techno-economic processes (hardware and software) for generating, sharing, developing and storing of information - has taprooted itself as a critical and indispensable set of tools which individuals, organisations, nations and regions can utilise in support to their comprehensive development objectives.

M. Castells, in his landmark work, *The Information Age: Economy, Society and Culture,* also similarly points out that knowledge and ICT are major driving forces of economic and social change. Knowledge is, and will remain, the lever of development as it gives mastery of ICT and the technology "embodies the capacity of societies to transform themselves," he says.

ICT enables people across the globe to source for, access and share, information. Nigerians are not excluded. Indeed, Nigerians in all sectors of the economy are engaged in serious exploration of how best to access and utilise the capabilities of ICTs to drive the production and distribution of goods and services, and also for the optimisation of social interaction and economic freedom.

ICT-enabled human and economic development is monumental. It has helped the developed world to significantly reduce the cost of business transactions. A deeper epistemological perspective of the frequent and rapid eclectic development and innovation of ICTs show that the technology has transformed human society from the information technology age to the knowledge age, an age driven mainly by deep and complex knowledge that has continued to shed light in areas hitherto thought to be beyond human cognition. From schools management to agricultural development, auditing, accounting, lawmaking, designing, oil exploration, healthcare management, manufacturing to crime control, the application of ICTs has become indispensable for quality assurance, goal attainment and cost effectiveness.

The maddening obsession for ICT innovation and development, especially in the developed countries, has and will continue to be guided and shaped with the "acute awareness" of the immense and increasing benefits of ICT-enabled socio-economic interconnectedness of countries and economic gains to organisations.

Infact, an elaborate ontology of ICTs as a rapid economic development enabler, shows that from the time when man's physical power was the driving engine of the economy to the age of the use of animal power and then, the industrial era, which was characterised by the resort to invention and use of mechanical power, and the current multi-complex computer age, none has been more productive in information sharing, cost effectiveness and production optimisation like the ICT development and deployment. Indeed, intellectual prophecies are already forecasting the deluge of the "computer brain" replacing human brain in the production chain in the next phase of ICT development.

Several scholars have also enhanced the view that the potential of ICTs to massively contribute to the development of socio-economic condition especially in developing economies has and will continue to stimulate overwhelming research and huge investments in all sectors of the economy globally. ICTs aspire to the realisation of the perceptions of desirable world order such as the United Nations' Millennium Development Goal of eradicating poverty.

It is pertinent to point out here that the intellectual pride and seeming obsession that have trailed ICT development, innovation and deployment, have been premised on the socio-economic development towards which it is intended to contribute. And this is majorly guided by the idea of society and economy as networks which conceptualise models of transformations happening in the contemporary world, and, now sipping massively into developing economies, stimulating massive ICT infrastructure development and investment.

The economic significance of ICT for development is, therefore, an undeniable one. It has remained a major instrument for economic, social and political gains especially in the area of e-governance which gives vent to efficiency, transparency and responsiveness.

The 2001 United Nations Development Programme (UNDP) report presents a clear association between technology and desirable development, pointing ICT, particularly the Internet, as a huge development enabler. The report which references a 1999 World Bank study reflects that

> technical progress accounted for between 40-50 per cent reduction in mortality spanning over four decades, that is, between 1960 and 1990 – making technology, indeed, ICT a more important source of gains than higher income or higher education levels among women.

The report also upholds the view that investment in ICT and its effective deployment and use, matter a lot for the economic development of a country. It is obvious that the potential of ICT to improve the performance of state institutions, health delivery and education, democratic participation, urban and regional planning and organisation, are inestimable.

Presently, the goals and objectives of the federal government of Nigeria are well-spelt out. And this begins from making ICTs not just only mandatory at every level of education in the country, but also an integral part of its reform agenda.

The federal government has already taken a cue from the global consensus that sustainable development is a process and not an end goal. This knowledge has made it mandatory for emerging economies to adopt the responsibility-proactive approach in ICT infrastructure development and deployment. The argument is that to sustain development, strong effort must be made to dull political rhetoric and enhance the application and optimisation of reliable and tested developmental tools. These ICT tools include the Internet, mobile phones, e-mails, microcomputers, among others.

Comprehensive and across-the-board ICT education for all is, therefore, an important starting point in any drive to catalyse national growth, using the platform of ICT. Whether it has to do with manipulating mobile phone handsets or surf the Internet in search of commodity prices or even to vote intelligently in e-elections, it is important that these foundational arrangements be put in place.

ICT education, therefore, to be most effective, must not be viewed as luxury or elective. Given the reality that a lot of business transactions in the world today, and far more going into the future, there must be agreement that providing ICT education for all is going to be a plus for the nation and society. So, no investment in that area should be regarded as superfluous or wasted. Indeed, going forward, the challenge really should be on how ICT can be used to create jobs, catalyse growth and save the future. We would return to these issues subsequently.

Sustainable Development: Two Decades On

In the words of **F.I. Anyasi,** the concept of economic growth and development has become a global crusade movement. He underscores the fact that this is indeed a process rather than an end or terminal goal. Maintaining a global socio-economic relevance and esteem amidst the growing complexities of governance and the challenges posed by ICT-forged globalisation, the Nigerian government was forced to integrate the application of ICTs in its developmental agenda.

ICTs are new technologies. But their revolutionising impact, especially in driving socio-economic growth and sustainable development in this current digital age, cannot be ignored or downplayed by any responsible government.

Sustainable development entails the application of reasoned actions that galvanises, promotes and upholds a "balance between resources used and generated...." It embodies the conscious and concrete efforts by a generation to pass the baton of socio-economic growth and development to the future generation.

This view was aptly crystalised by H. Imam who noted that there are three main pillars upon which sustainable growth and development stands, namely, economic development, social development and environmental protection. Re-echoing the covenants of the United Nations Conference on Environment and Development, Imam argues that the catalysing strength that propels these pillars towards achieving the needed rapid and efficient development includes, *inter alia*, qualitative management of education and capacity building.

Relevant literature on ICT development, deployment and diffusion show that its revolutionising power lies not only in the technologies capacity to "instantaneously connect vast networks of individuals and organisations across great geographical distances at very little cost," thus, breaking down the walls and barriers across countries, but mainly in its capacity to transmit and retain authentic knowledge which has remained the engine of socio-economic growth and sustainable development globally.

ICT technology, through the Internet, allows secured access to digital content thereby facilitating the flow of information, capital, ideas, people and products. These have led to massive transformation of businesses, markets and organisations, revolutionising learning and knowledge sharing, empowering citizens and communities and creating significant socio-economic growth in many countries and enhancing the realisation of concrete growth and developmental projections.

It is obvious that there have been rising optimism and concern for sustainable patterns and processes of development in Nigeria since independence in 1960. This is because of the perception that the texture and characteristics of policies, methods and projects by government tend to lean more on mere political stakes instead of weighty economic considerations which guarantee better future and equitable outcomes. This deliberate subordination of economic considerations under political dribbles, dulled and retarded all the development plans initiated by successive governments for several years.

Although ICT gained rapid global recognition and prominence beginning from the early 1990s, Nigeria's bold step to embrace it did not begin until a decade later. Indeed, Nigeria's ICT policy implementation only gained foothold when the Federal Executive Council (FEC), in April 2001, approved the establishment of the National Information Technology Development Agency (NITDA).

NITDA, by the policy, was empowered to chart the roadmap for Nigeria's ICT highway "making Nigeria IT capable country in Africa and a key player in the information society through using ICTs as an engine for Sustainable Development and global competitive-ness". The policy enables the agency to search out, collaborate and enter into strategic alliance and joint ventures with the private sector operators in a bid to realise its objectives which are to

1. establish and develop ICT infrastructure and maximise its use nationwide;
2. create ICT awareness and ensure universal access in promoting ICT diffusion in all sectors of national life;
3. create an enabling environment and facilitate private sector (national and multinational) investment in ICT;
4. ensure that ICT resources are readily available to promote efficient national development;
5. guarantee that the country benefits maximally and contributes meaningfully by providing the global solutions to the challenges of the information age;
6. empower the youth with ICT skills and prepare them for global competitiveness;
7. encourage government and private sector joint venture collaboration;
8. empower Nigerians to participate in software and ICT development;
9. develop human capital with emphasis on creating and supporting a knowledge-based society;
10. build a mass pool of ICT literate manpower using the NYSC and other platforms as a train-the-trainer scheme for capacity building;
11. encourage local production and manufacture of ICT components in a competitive manner, and
12. integrate ICT into the mainstream of education and training.

With the incorporation of ICT into Nigeria's development process, in less than a decade and half, ICT penetration and diffusion, especially the mobile phone and the Internet, have remained one of the fastest growing in the world. Now, corporate organisations, especially financial institutions, schools and schools' examination bodies, MDAs, hospitals, courts, states and the federal government, are connected in a complex web of ICT-enabled network. This has boosted the transmission and sharing of digital content knowledge like e-mails, virtual libraries, etc. Indeed, Nigeria, through the forces of ICT, "a huge wave of information, travelling through the information superhighway", has enlisted as a member of this globalised society in which knowledge and its access are "commodities as important as land, capital and labour".

Due to the dynamics of social change and the realisation that education is a potent instrument for solving present and future challenges, the government resolved and introduced ICTs into the school system through the National Policy on Education. The federal government provides the basic infrastructure and training for the realisation of this goal at all levels of the education system.

Bassey *et al* report that the applications of ICTs in school management have considerably reduced the growing complexities that characterise secondary and tertiary schools administration thereby enabling quality assurance and goal attainment.

From the transfer, lodgment and withdrawal of cash in banks to the collation of election results, compiling and release of West Africa Examination Council (WAEC) results, marketing of e-newspaper to shopping and hiring of labour, the introduction and application of ICTs in Nigeria's socio-economic milieu has been solidly entrenched as an enabler and an accelerant of growth and sustainable development in the country.

Globalisation and the ICT Gap

There is a yawning ICT gap between the developed, developing and underdeveloped countries of the world. Morales-Gomez and Melesse hold the strong view that a country's capacity to effectively and efficiently position itself as a producer and/or a consumer of knowledge in the current information age, determines how far apart she will be on the ladder of social and economic development. Deepening the thoughts of Morals-Gomez and Melesse, Avgerou has elevated Thomson's view on Escobar's Foucauldian critiques of the "discourse on development and voiced suspicion about the nature of development transformation towards which ICT is understood to contribute". He crystallises his view on the acute awareness that ICT development, innovation and advancement have been mainly driven by the economies of the first world – primarily North America and Europe – and the increasing socio-economic interconnectedness of all countries and regions through a cobweb of ICT tools and artifacts in a condition called globalisation which has created stiff competitiveness in a global free market. He argues that difficulties erupt following trends and standards of this ICT-forced globalisation which, with the "limited technology and skills available in developing countries or regions", created a new form of "digital divide" which has given vent to a form of inequality and socio-economic disadvantage.

Beyond the superordinate and subordinate socio-economic complex created by ICT-enabled globalisation, it is apt to note that there is a gradual demolition of the national and regional cultures that have been historically formed and rooted in "developing" and "underdeveloped" countries. On this perspective of the nature of ICT-driven development transformation, Avgerou evolves the theory of progressive transformation and disruptive transformation. He avers that ICT catalysing strength for transformation in most cases conflicts with, rather than fit into, the culture of the predominant social milieu. These, he notes, contribute to widening the ICT gap or "digital divide".

Studies of ICT growth and development in the last two decades provide insight on how the abnormal obsession and frequency of innovations of ICT tools and artifacts by the advanced economies, has continued to slow down the catch-up race by developing economies like Nigeria. This has put developing economies in such a disadvantaged position and relationship as ICT origin and rapidity in innovation tend to make developing countries perpetual consumers of ICT tools and artifacts.

Layers upon layers of studies show that the digital divide may continue to grow. For example, Sahlfeld, in a review of how ICTs work for development, observes that record of foreign investment and aid to developing countries to build ICT infrastructure are mainly motivated by self interest.

> Be it individual communication via telephone or mass communications via radio and television broadcasting - private sector investments and western govern-mental aid would materialize only if profits are in reach ....

This has led to the non-development of comprehensive landline telephone infrastructure.

ICT and Emerging Economies: Bird's Eye View of ICT Development in India

Globally, ICT is recognised and accepted as a catalysing agent that can stimulate national progress and socio-economic transformation. This insight has motivated most future-looking developing countries like India to make and entrench regulations and policies that ensure wide access for her citizens and greater participation in ICT development by her increasing and vibrant workforce.

India's ICT market has been the fastest growing in the world, spanning over one and half decades in rapid growth and development. This feat has, therefore, recommended it as a desirable model from which Nigeria can glean some lessons.

In contradistinction to Nigeria's ICT policy which gained foothold in 2001, literature regarding the nature of ICT development, deployment, growth and diffusion process in India demonstrates that the country's ambitious ICT policy dates back to 1988. But the major giant stride on her ICT roadmap was made in 1994 when the government introduced the national telecoms policy. This was followed with the new telecoms policy of 1999 and the broadband policy of 2004. With such a policy framework and a liberal business environment that conduces to predictable socio-economic growth and development, India's quantum leap in ICT innovation gained ascendancy. India is now a global powerhouse in software production and export in the ICT industry. Her mark in software production and development has been helped and boosted by the government in many ways. First was the development of software technology parks, extension of incentives in the form of tax breaks to many of the companies in the industry to help promote and optimise sustainable growth. These gave vent to an avalanche of foreign direct investments (FDIs) in the industry.

Agreed that India's hardware industry growth remained sluggish for some years as a result of sundry trade barriers, tariffs and government protective policies, but it has begun to experience a great lease of production life and has solidly stamped India as one of the emerging powerhouses in hardware production and export.

In studies of ICT development and implementation in India, Sumontro silently identifies and notes focus, favourable policies and the hunger of the large pool of labour to succeed, as some of the major driving forces behind the success story of ICT growth and development in India.

India's outsourcing sector has remained the world's largest and is largely dominated by ICT services, playing significant roles in the country's overall economic outlook. The Indian offshore ICT and business-process-outsourcing industry generates approximately $31 billion annually with a workforce of nearly 3,000,000. And in the last half decade, the industry has accounted for 9-11 percent of the country's GDP.

India's resolve to continue to expand and sustain the industry's growth and development to the next generation of ICTs has generally triggered a new wave of enthusiasm in the industry. Jaideep Mehta, the Vice President and Country General Manager, IDC India, said that

> 2014 will finally see the India IT eco-system begin a serious transition to the third platform technologies of cloud and mobility, and to a lesser

extent big data, and social. IDC predicts the influx of cloud and enterprise mobility technologies along with the associated changes in architecture and IT management processes.

Despite the huge progress being made in ICT outsourcing in India, Sumontro's findings show that the diffusion and penetration of ICTs have been heavily hampered by the country's caste system culture, hilly villages and poor disposable income. The study also catalogues the sundry challenges plaguing India's ICT sector as follows:

1. Inability of the IT services and ITES-BPO industries to maintain and share common infrastructural facilities across institutions.
2. Shortage of skilled faculty for providing relevant, industry-oriented training.
3. Inadequate industry exposure.
4. Increasing discrepancy between the education focus and the quality of skills developed at top-tier educational institutions and other private and public centres of learning.
5. Lack of correlation and synchronisation between the existing technical education system and industry requirements: absence of adequate academia-industry linkages.
6. Rigidities in the curriculum and evaluation system.

ICT as Solution: The Nigerian Experience

We discussed the need to ensure that ICT contributes maximally in solving Nigeria's core challenges of growing the economy, creating jobs and saving our future. What is left is to make concrete proposals that would push us in this direction.

A few years ago, the federal government signed on to a Computer-for-All Initiative. Scores of computers were bought for civil servants and there was also talk of government promoting a $100 laptop for people within the educational system. This scheme ran for a while but it has since floundered. We need a revamped version of it today. In our view, there were two basic problems with that scheme. One was that it relied almost exclusively on government funding. In an environment where government funds are sparse and insufficient and with a lot of interests competing to get more and more of it, this has not really worked. Also is the fact that the scheme's deliverables were too short-sighted and ill-focused. Computers were being given to people without computer literacy and who had not been sufficiently prepared to appreciate this new mosaic. There was little motivation.

What we propose now is the establishment of a Foundation for ICT Awareness and Development. This scheme should run as a public-private partnership, as a foundation that would take as its objective the mobilisation and preparation of Nigerians to benefit maximally from the ICT age. These would come in a number of areas:

Job Creation

The number of people to be recruited to ensure that the goal of providing comprehensive nationwide ICT education is met, is indeed massive. Already, a few ICT courses have presently been introduced into the school system while a number of people have already been engaged as instructors in the process. When we take it to another level, the employment benefits will indeed be exponential.

Boosting the Outsourcing Sub-Sector

India and a few other states have presently benefited massively from ICT outsourcing. We too can. Low cost of labour and technological competence are needed here and the task then would be to work on the security and motivation systems. Infact, properly motivated, this could be accompanied with some pressure in the form of a revamped security on the abusers of ICT in the country. This is because a strong ICT platform must be secure and customer-friendly.

Final thoughts

Is ICT part of the Nigerian reality today? Yes, it is. But more often than not, it is the negative transmutations of it that has been most widespread. In this, readers are familiar with the sceptre of the infamous but globally recognised "Nigerian internet scam artists" otherwise referred to as the "Yahoo yahoo boys". However, beyond its present form and structure, the presence of this phenomenon is basically symptomatic of the fact that we already have enough of our population who really appreciate, in their own misguided way, the enormous potential of ICT to lift individuals and societies out of their socio-economic limitations and conditions. We must then take steps to redress this reverse potential in such a way as to ensure a lawful and more complimentary win-win situation for both "the boys" and the nation.

Concerted action is required at the state, local government and federal levels if we are to take the right steps and get the anticipated results that we desire. What we are calling for then is the establishment of cross-cutting technology development centres across the nation. With a central coordinating centre at the national level (which must be active, not bureaucratic), such a centre should be engaged in continuous market and policy review with a view to taking maximum advantage of shifts in trends and developments within this immensely mobile and most dynamic sector. It cannot be anyway else.

To boost the effectiveness base of the national coordinating centre, we also propose the establishment of a semi-regulatory and cross-cutting private sector-driven National ICT Development Foundation. Such an establishment which we propose should be composed of ICT sector players. Representatives of big business donor interests and government regulators would help to catalyse the much-needed critical action in the area of projects conception, finance mobilisation, research and development and multi-sectoral networking. The foundation should drive on all fours. And it should be invested with power to take quick and swift decisions in the interest of the nation's ICT development.

For firms and individuals that would support the foundation's work particularly in the critical area of finance, it should come with some benefits. For example, corporate bodies should be encouraged to contribute to, and/or invest in, the scheme using a tax-deductible framework. But even beyond this, they should be equally encouraged to take advantage of, and collaborate with, the foundation and centre even in their own individual ICT needs.

To get the centre and foundation to properly deliver on its mandate, care must be taken to ensure that its personnel are top-range and properly motivated. The coordinators must be chosen on an internationally competitive framework and given all that they need to succeed.

Going down the line, the scheme should be cross-cutting and run from local to federal tiers of government, and across the nursery to university sectors of the educational system. As a nation, we should begin to think in terms of *computer-speak* and prepare the ground for the next Nigerian billionaires who will be coming from our own silicon valley. Zinox boss, Leo Stan Ekeh, and his contemporary at Omatek, Florence Seriki, are examples of computer whizzkids who have made it good in our environment today. But they are not enough. And we need and should get more.

To achieve our ICT goals overall, we must emphasise the imperative of government support in the area of patronage, mobilisation and lobby. In this, we commend the example of RLG in Ghana where support from the government has enabled a small-time business centre operator as Roland Agambire to blossom into a tech whizzkid with international tentacles. It can also be done here. And better too!

6

Improving the Nation's Education System

As an avid reader of autobiographies, especially of living legends, it has helped me connect the dots about aspects of their lives that have remained a mystery and, of course, today also creates an added opportunity for follow-up questions especially where the dots do not seem connect well. *My Journey: As the Future becomes the Past,* which chronicles the life of Dr. Udo Udo-Aka up to the present time, is an interesting read. It is a 424 page book, rich in narratives that is recommend to all who are interested in developing the dogged determination to succeed in life and in the process offer selfless service to their communities, be it local, global or virtual. The following comment by Dr. Udo Udo-Aka calls for attention and will be discussed in greater detail.

> In my part of Nigeria, people of my generation and those before, due to lack of western education, had been handicapped by the glaring lack of records of events, and achievement of our forebears.

Education

For the avoidance of doubt, western education is extremely important. In today's global village, the level of its preponderance, if applied in the right way, tends to dictate how competitive individuals and communities become. However, not all important education is western. More than ever, "as the future becomes the past",[1] we see a need to formalise and manage the education of tradesmen, craftsmen, artisans, small and medium-sized entrepreneurs and

---

[1]   Udo Udo-Aka (2014). *My Journey: As the future becomes the past.* Mayfive Media.

many other players in the economy. Increasingly, because of the way our society has evolved and the value system that seems to prevail, we are at the stage where we ponder on how to formally educate people even on matters of social etiquette and acceptable public conduct. This will be the focus of this chapter.

The Role of Education

Education is one of the most important tools for building strong and vibrant nations. Education must be seen by government as investment and not a fiscal liability. Experiences in other parts of the world, both in developed and emerging economies, have proved conclusively that knowledge and skill are a form of capital, and this capital is a product of deliberate and skilled investment in education. Experiences in a number of western countries have indicated that an increase in national output is a direct result of investment in human capital. Qualitative education and skills training, by the way, are investments that can be made in human capital. The question, therefore, is: What are the specific roles of education in society? The following quickly come to mind, namely,

1. Education helps prepare the individual for life. This preparation involves the transfer of knowledge, skills and values from generation to generation, country to country and individual to individual. Through education, we gain expertise in our field of interest and are equipped to provide value to others and in the process make a living.
2. Education creates a pool of knowledge and develops future fields of exploration that help to drive innovation and progress in society. This, generally, engenders better amenities for living that offers better quality of life.
3. Education helps to create enlightened societies and build people necessary to run the public and private institutions that promote social cohesion and economic well-being. Through education, a nation develops a pool of professionals such as lawyers, engineers, bankers. etc.
4. Education creates enlightenment. Through education, we experience and understand how societies interact in other

climes and gain insights into our history in order to make sense of the future.

5. Education is crucial to development. Tons of research papers and studies exist to demonstrate the empirical causalities between education as one variable and others such as economic development, food security, social welfare, rule of law, human capital accumulation, etc.

Education can be formal as administered through the school system in Nigeria which is currently anchored on the soon-to-be phased out 6-3-3-4 system (the 9-3-4 system has been proposed to take off soon) and other vocational training institutes, or informal, by way of the instructions received from family members and friends, as we pass through life. Both systems are threatened. But our present focus is on the formal education system in Nigeria.

Education Administration in Nigeria

There are three stages of formal education in Nigeria: primary, secondary and tertiary. Funding and management of the different levels fall under different tiers of government. Of course, there is the *almajiri* system which addresses the need of itinerant or nomadic children in northern Nigeria. This is a hybrid of Islamic/limited western education.

The federal government recognises the importance of education in national development and has demonstrated this awareness through the budgetary allocation to education issues which took up an average of 7.1 percent in the last few years. In 2014, the allocation to education accounted for 10.7 percent or ₦493 billion ($3.1 billion) of the federal budget, an increase of 15 percent from 2013. Education has always ranked in the top three sectors that receive the highest allocation from the budget.

Additionally, the federal government has promoted the establishment of universities, owns the unity schools for secondary education and spends an additional 2 percent from its Consolidated Revenue Fund to support the states and local governments in the provision of basic education at the primary and junior secondary school levels. In view of the commitment to spend this quantum of money, the question is: "Has the educational system achieved the roles enumerated earlier?"

Primary Education

Public primary education is covered under the federal government promoted Universal Basic Education programme that guarantees nine years of free primary and junior secondary education to every child in Nigeria. The policy was muted in 1999 but became effective after the passage of the enabling law in 2004. Children are expected to start primary school at age six and spend six years in it before proceeding to junior secondary school for a further three years. The cost of the primary education is borne by the local government authorities who are also charged with the administration, sometimes supported by the state governments.

In truth, public primary education is shunned by all who can afford private primary education for their children. The problem, however, goes beyond the public-private school dichotomy.

Education for All (EFA), a monitoring arm of UNESCO, noted in a 2011 report that globally, 61 million children of primary school age do not have access to education while 10.5 million or 17.21 percent are Nigerian children. These kids are engaged in street trading, domestic servitude or helping their parents in the farm. The *almajiri* system, which dates back many centuries in northern Nigeria is also not working as the supervising clerics have encouraged the children to undertake street begging for sustenance.

Going by the report from the education section of the US Embassy in Nigeria,[2] the incidence of non-attendance is highest in the North East and North West, especially Borno State, where an estimated 72 percent of children are not enrolled in school. Recent events in that state and region point to one of the consequences of lack of education in a society.

---

[2]   Education Section, United States Embassy in Nigeria, Nigerian Education Fact Sheet, 2012.

Acquiring sound primary education is the bedrock of success in all other levels and the failures being witnessed in imparting knowledge, funding, enrollment, etc, has gone a long way in affecting the quality of input to other levels.

Secondary Education

Public secondary education is solely funded by the state governments except for the unity schools which are funded by the federal government. At this stage, there is the critical problem of "access" to public secondary education. Statistics are difficult to come by in this sector but the most recent one, which is a 2006 publication from the New Roadmap for Nigeria's educational sector, puts the number of public secondary schools nationwide at 7,129 and the situation has not changed much. This situation has created a fertile ground for private secondary schools, many of which provide education of doubtful quality.

The reason for the lower rates of enrollment is not surprising. There is the big issue of "planning education". As pointed out above, there were 7,129 secondary schools across the country as at 2006. The same report also noted that there were 54,434 primary schools in the country at the same time, almost eight times the number of secondary schools. The big questions are: What did we plan to do with the graduates of the 54,434 primary schools? Did we intend they continued education or did we intend that they stopped at that level of schooling? In 2006 alone, we saw that the number in secondary schools was only half the number that enrolled in primary schools.

Tertiary Education

The funding of tertiary education and the public university system rests on the state and federal governments which established them in the first place. As at 2012, there were 69 universities, 44 polytechnics and 37 colleges of education. The proliferation of universities within a short period has created its own problem of developing faculty quick enough and of the right quality to ensure that real teaching, learning and research takes place. The stories one is regaled with by current and recent graduates indicate that very little learning actually goes on there. As the CEO of one of the largest employers of labour, the experience from sitting-in on sessions where the display by these graduates in their subject areas has been disappointing. Perhaps, in recognition of the shortcomings of our tertiary institutions, there has been a flight of children of the rich and other top students who can secure scholarships to other countries. In 2010, Nigeria was the 17th largest source of international undergraduate students and the 19th largest source of international graduate students. Readily available statistics show that as at 2010, about 6,568 Nigerian students were enrolled in 733 American universities and enjoyed $5.5 million in one form of aid or the other.

As we seek to expand the number of tertiary institutions to accommodate the number being churned out from the secondary school system, focus has to bear on hard issues like funding, modernising curricula in areas that are most relevant to society and the development of faculty.

Issues with the Education System in Nigeria

There are myriad issues with the educational system in Nigeria. Some of them have already been discussed. Facing these squarely, however, the following are some of the areas that need urgent attention and which hopefully should begin to address the rot in the system:

Funding and Administration

As pointed out earlier, ₦493 billion or 10.7 percent of the national budget was voted to address public education in Nigeria. Out of this, 83 percent was for recurrent expenditure (payment of salaries, etc) while 17 percent was committed to other areas. Education share of state budgets is even less. While there are now probably more private schools than public schools, especially at the primary and secondary levels of education, the importance of public education cannot be downplayed. Private education remains very expensive and, as can be seen, 32 percent of drop-outs at the primary level do so because of the high cost of education.

Second, there are just not enough primary and secondary schools in the country. This, perhaps, has to do with funding and administration. Take, for instance, primary schools that are to be funded mainly by the local governments. A visit to local government offices, perhaps, with the exception of some in Lagos State, will show that the skill and commitment level of those who are councillors and chairmen that administer the local governments are suited for purposes other than super-intending over primary schools funding and administration. Many schools across the country are dilapidated and run down and, even in this century, there are many Nigerian communities where learning takes place under trees.

Stepping up to higher learning, we see serious funding challenges that have virtually crippled the universities. In 2013, university lecturers, under the aegis of Academic Staff Union of Universities (ASUU), were on strike for about six months because of a dispute with the federal government over wages, retirement age for professors, research grants etc. While these look like reasonable demands, which if met could go to improve commitment of lecturers, the bigger question is: "Is this a sustainable means of funding tertiary education in the country in view of current shortfalls in the level of finance needed and dwindling federal revenues?"

Enrollment

Enrollment figures for all levels of education are low compared to the population of eligible children. The reasons for this are varied. At the primary and secondary levels, the challenge is to build interest amongst parents to register their children and wards for school in the face of the difficulties in achieving this. Results have been mixed in different parts of the country with enrollment being typically high in the southern part of the country and low in the northern part. Religion, culture and poverty have been reinforcing factors for this trend, but difficulties in accessing schools and lack of awareness have also played a role.

At the tertiary level, the seemingly low enrollment figure is for a different reason. There are simply not enough tertiary institutions to serve the teeming population of students who sit for entrance examinations every year. In April 2014, a total of 1,030,252 candidates tested for less than 100,000 spaces in the Unified Tertiary Matriculation Examinations.

Obviously, to educate more Nigerians, the strategy to drive up enrollment and meet the Millennium Development Goal target for education which is that "by 2015, all Nigerian children (boys and girls) can complete a full course of primary schooling and the literacy of 15-24 years old females and males will be high", should be reviewed to make it more effective.

Curriculum and Learning Methods

For education to be meaningful and relevant to both the individual and the nation, the embedded curriculum must be current, address specific needs of that level of education and in general should be such that individuals are able to use it to advance themselves and society. We need to question the age of curriculum and teaching methods in public schools at all levels in view of the advances made in the private schools and the seeming outstanding success of products of these public schools. More and more, we see less academic prize winners from the public institutions and the questions should be "why?"

Furthermore, looking at the curriculum in the colonial and post-colonial era, it would appear that not much has changed. Does this curriculum, especially at the tertiary level, produce the knowledge base that will address our needs as a nation? As an emerging economy, have we sat down to evaluate the needs of the economy in terms of engineers, scientists, doctors, mathematicians, etc? Have we developed an incentive to attract people to these disciplines and a curriculum that addresses our specific needs as a country? Are our curriculum and institutions developing finished products who are best suited for white collar jobs or are we focused on building and developing the next generation of entrepreneurs? What we see around us are symptoms of a failed educational system[3] such as

---

[3]   Akinlua Akinsola. Driving curriculum content and practice in higher education in Nigeria towards relevance: Reforming higher education in Africa.

a. unemployment among graduates of tertiary institutions;
b. low level of knowledge and "know how" in areas of specialization;
c. poor ability to express oneself in both written and spoken English Language.

It is most certain that the root cause of the first point above is because the system is churning out graduates whose skills are in very low demand in the Nigerian economy.

Lecturers/Teachers

Recently, a primary school teacher in Edo State failed a basic reading test randomly administered by the Governor. A subsequent attempt by the Governor to do skills assessment of primary school teachers was unsuccessful because of a boycott by the teachers and threat to go on strike if the Governor persisted with the idea. This is not an isolated case as attempts in Ekiti State to also take stock of the skills and knowledge of her teachers have met with stiff resistance.

There is no doubt that the quality of teachers is poor across all levels of education and teaching has become a last resort for those, trained and untrained, who are not able to secure jobs in other sectors of the economy. Take, for instance, the proliferation of universities across the country in such a short time. While funding will prove a major issue, a more debilitating one will be the lack of faculty to man these institutions or to put it more succinctly, the use of charlatans to carry out research and provide instruction in these universities.

Effects of No or Low Quality Education

Poverty

Lack of education or poor quality education is a chief contributor to poverty. The results of a Gallup research on poverty in sub-Saharan Africa published in 2012 indicated that, at the least, a good secondary school education was necessary for residents of this region of the world to live above poverty. Its findings showed that 85 percent of those who had only primary school education or partial secondary school education are not meaningfully employed. We do not need to go far to validate these results as evidence is all around us.

Unemployment

The economic stagnation of recent years and the attendant high unemployment rates have become reinforcing loops that the country will struggle to break free from. The National Population Commission (NPC) notes that 24 percent of Nigerians are unemployed while the National Bureau for Statistics (NBS) goes further to reveal that 54 percent of young people are unemployed. The educational causes for unemployment are manifold, ranging from outright illiteracy, products of our educational system who really are not educated, to graduates whose skills and knowledge are not relevant to the needs of the Nigerian economy. Unemployment itself comes with many other complementary ills in the society such as crime and social disorder.

Crime

The uneducated mind is open to, and accepts, many influences without questioning. A lack of education leads to unemploy-ment, poverty and consequently dependency on third parties for basic needs and survival. This population subset has become a fertile recruitment pool for crime, political violence and religious extremism. These have become an albatross on the nation's social and economic growth. The earlier we took action to offer formal or alternative education for the mass of young ones, the better it will be for the country and the rest of us.

Low Economic Development

Education promotes economic development In a recent World Bank article,[4] the authors established a link between quantity/quality of education and economic growth in countries. Cumulative years of research from other scholars have proved conclusively that education has both direct and indirect effects on national output. Educated workers raise national income directly because schooling raises their

---

[4]   E.A. Hanushek and L. Wobmann. Education quality and economic growth. World Bank,

marginal productivity. They affect national income indirectly by increasing the marginal productivity of physical capital and of other workers. The challenge then for our policy makers and education managers is how to integrate this knowledge in planning.

Lack of National Competitiveness

The quality of individuals in an economy determines the productivity and, ultimately, the national competitiveness of such countries. Recently, Nigeria rebased her economy and emerged with an enlarged size of US$509 billion. With this, it dwarfed the South African economy in absolute size. What remained unsaid was that with this new figure, our GDP per capita (which is more relevant for comparative purposes) increased to an estimated US$3,029, which is just under half of South Africa's 2013 GDP per capita of US$7,352. We need to keep this in mind. Even with her recent challenges, that country remains a more productive country. Good quality education improves individual productivity which cascades to improved national productivity.

Indeed, there are many other negative outcomes associated with lack of education or low quality education. But we have just touched on the ones which we consider the more obvious ones and which we see and feel around us every day.

How to Overhaul the Current System

Many experts have studied the problem with our educational system and have come up with research reports, white papers, etc, on how this can be fixed. Let us join the fray and focus on what could be considered to be low hanging fruits that can have immediate impact. They are not unconnected with the challenges identified earlier.

Driving up Enrollment

We can achieve this by creating awareness for the benefits of education and giving bite to the compulsory free education policy. How come that we see children of school age hawking on the streets or engaging in other domestic work during school hours without any government organ raising eyebrows. We also need to get public schools closer to the people because in many cases, that could be the only affordable means of education. Government needs to fashion out a carrot and stick approach to get parents to actually send their children to school.

Funding to be Expanded

Already, the budgetary allocation to education by the federal government and some state governments indicate that they recognise it as very important. First, with funding, we should ensure that the monies voted for education are actually spent on education. Second, we should ensure that every naira spent is optimised and that means making sure it is spent in a way it creates the most impact. Funding needs to be expanded but in view of dwindling government revenue (by the way, they need to spend time figuring out why revenue is dwindling and work on it quickly) and other competing priorities, the reality is that government needs to find a way to engage the private sector in education funding. An approach which could have worked was the "Adopt a School" programme introduced by the education minister during the closing months of the Obasanjo administration.

Curriculum and Administration of Schools

At the least, public primary schools should be solely administered by the state governments. It is too much of a serious business to be left at the whims and caprices of local councils as most councils in many states do not have the manpower or motivation to manage an excellent system. Across all levels of education, there should be constant review and development of curriculum to ensure that these are relevant to the development of enlightened individuals and productive nation.

Prioritising Knowledge and Competences

As a developing country, we need to decide on the knowledge, skills and competences needed to actualise all the visions about greatness that is commonplace now. Disciplines such as entrepreneurship studies, mathematics, science and technology should be high on that list.

Developing Strong Regulatory Framework

The government should also have a very strong regulatory arm to monitor the quality of education in private schools. In the early post-independence days, we had the ever present education inspectors who went from school to school to monitor academic activities. If this is still in existence, then the role needs to be strengthened. Otherwise, there is an urgent need to re-introduce it.

Expanding Our Education Infrastructure

Closely related to the issue of funding is the need to expand our education infrastructure. Currently, recurrent expenditure consumes about 83 percent of the budgetary allocation to education. This is, perhaps, why we still see pictures of dilapidated classrooms and children learning under trees or sitting on the floors to be taught. At the least, our public schools should compete favourably with the private schools in the provision of infrastructure. It is difficult to imagine how any learning goes on in the schools captured by the images above.

Teaching the Teachers

This, perhaps, will be the most difficult one to achieve even though it is clear to all that there is a dearth of quality teachers/lecturers across all levels of schooling. They are members of very powerful unions who see any attempt at skills and knowledge assessment as a prelude to mass sacks and are ready to scuttle this. Nevertheless, it is imperative that we do the skills assessment in order to know where remedial action is needed. There is no doubt that even if every other thing is in place and we do not have the right people teaching in our schools, we would have made little progress. This is an area we have to grapple with and it will involve having the right incentives in place to attract and keep the right people teaching. My suspicion is that to be successful here, we need to ensure that the teachers' rewards are right here on earth and enjoy this on a daily basis.

Ordinarily, to change a system is a tough call for anybody. Changing the education system will be tougher. While the best time to start was yesterday, the next best time is today. It is something we must do if this country is to have any meaningful future.

7

Nigeria, Your Glass is Half Empty

You may have heard this story before. Two people were asked to look at a glass that had only half of its liquid content. They were then requested to take positions: whether the glass was half-full or half-empty. It is the paradox of Nigeria today. Our glass appears half-empty! This is not pessimism; far from it. All is possible in this great country. But Nigeria epitomises the parable of the ostrich that buries its head in the sand oblivious of the fact that its larger frame is visible for all to see. The first place to begin in getting to be "all that God has called us to be", is to tell ourselves the bitter truth no matter how inconvenient.

Even when we demur from saying it as it is, it, however, still gets said. Early in 2014, while the nation was basking in the euphoria that her GDP rebasing exercise had ensured that it had pulled ahead of her biggest rival on the continent, South Africa, the news also came that thousands of job seekers who had besieged job centres created by the Nigeria Immigration Service had been involved in a stampede which left many dead and several more injured. The rebasing exercise, desirable as it was, has since been concluded, confirming that on account of her large population, natural resource endowments and the tenacity of her peoples, Nigeria is today the biggest economy on the continent and the 26th largest economy in the world. Yet, young people die on queues while waiting for jobs that are simply not there. The ostrich gets caught. Nigeria, the glass is half-empty.

Wanted: A Nigerian Marshall Plan

For about six years of World War II, the forces of the "free world" had battled against the armies of fascism to ensure that a nefarious ideology did not succeed in putting all of humanity under jackboots. The free world prevailed but it was at a huge cost. Millions died. Nations were destroyed, relationships fractured, with further costs later on. Nations had to be rebuilt. People needed to be re-energised. And importantly, vanquished armies, nations and peoples had to be demobilised, re-integrated and changed. Massive resources were required and the challenge fell on the American-led Allied Forces to put in place a reconstruction programme, hence the genesis of the world-famous Marshall plan.

At the foundation of the rebuilding programme in Nigeria would be a return to the basics. And at the apex here is the nation's educational system. Indeed, the state of education in Nigeria today is very worrisome. Statistics from the United Nations Education, Scientific and Cultural Organisation (UNESCO) show that Nigeria currently has about 10 million children of school age out of the educational loop. Furthermore, up the chain, only a negligible number of children who enrolled in primary schools finally make the transition to secondary.

But the ultimate challenge is to be found at the tertiary level. Here, education first problem is cultural: many young people in Nigeria have been nurtured to believe that they cannot make a way in life without tertiary education. But this is not exactly true as the world's two richest entrepreneurs today, Bill Gates and Carlos Slim Helu, are not university graduates. Even here in Nigeria, and by extension, in large swathes of Africa, many successful people do not have a formal tertiary education.

Equally, young Nigerians are faced with the contradiction that the society that so viscerally encourages them to pursue tertiary education has done a terrible job of opening up opportunities for the actualisation of this desire. And so, year after year, hundreds of thousands of candidates flock to seek admission for the few spaces that the system can offer. As is evident, it is this unthinking incapacity that, more than any other factor, has promoted the current situation where tens of thousands of Nigerian tertiary education seekers emigrate from the country in search of educational opportunities from which only a handful eventually return.

Another challenge with education at the tertiary level has to do with a lack of commitment and attention to quality. Routinely, Nigerian university lecturers and their counterparts in polytechnics and other such establishments go on strike with very little concerted intervention by the political authorities. In 2013, for example, one such strike by university lecturers lasted for more than five months. Even at this time of writing, another strike by polytechnic teachers has exposed the sector's weak underbelly.

Within such a climate and on account of a canvas that is laden with unqualified and poorly remunerated teaching personnel as well as the absence of critical teaching aids and requisite learning infrastructure, only a handful of super-motivated students that the system ultimately pronounces as "graduates" can fit into the nation's competitive labour market. But it need not be so. Through generations, the difference between one civilisation and the other has been the quality and content of its education and enterprise. From ancient Egypt, through Sumeria, Rome, Europe and today's leading nations in North America and Asia, this has been a sure given.

Today, however, decades of crude and corrupt politicking has taken its toll on the educational enterprise in Nigeria. Across the land, the nation is confronted by many failings, with one of the most notable being the spectre of teachers that have themselves not been properly taught! When the blind leads the blind, all inevitably fall into a ditch. There are other challenges: infrastructure, poor remuneration, content and finance.

Put succinctly, the nation has to muster all of her will to fix this problem. Education is too fundamental to be trifled with. As keen Nigerian observers have noted, the alternative to the robust educational system is a continued perpetuation of widespread ignorance, lack of properly skilled manpower, non-productivity and under-development.

What is needed, therefore, is a very determined intervention that would get to the root of addressing all of the rot that presently exists within the system, preferably, in one fell swoop.

Some years ago, Nobel laureate Professor Wole Soyinka, a former university don himself, made this point when he advocated the total closure of all of the nation's universities so that the nation freshly re-assesses the subject of what makes a university. Without going as far as shutting down tertiary institutions, we think that at the core of the challenge is the critical issue of understanding, once again and defining, simply but properly, what end education should be. This is because, on account of poor planning and improper matching of content and expected results, the resources presently being deployed in funding education are, to put it frankly, wasted. Within this context then, every course in tertiary institutions should ultimately produce graduates the country needs and yearns for. The present situation in the sector is largely reactionary and defensive. What we need is fresh and renewed thinking.

There is also the very critical issue of ensuring that any educational reform does not only deal with the problems of tertiary education but also squarely addresses the problems of primary and secondary institution.

Finally, but certainly not least importantly, is the issue of funding. A local Nigerian adage avers that preparation of good soup costs money. It is a misnomer in every material sense for us to continue to expect that the current system will by some act of faith deliver to us high quality educational standard, when we have not supported the system with well-motivated staff, the appropriate complement of infrastructure and technology and the right calibre of teachable students who will deliver the expected goods.

Structural, not Adhoc

As has been suggested for the educational sector, we must proceed to the imperative of rebuilding Nigeria in a structural, systematic, organised and efficient manner. Again, it is simply not enough to draw copious intellectual plans on what is to be done. We must equally proceed in a most resolute manner to walk our talk. When we talk about structural change, we mean change that is methodical and aligned. This must take into consideration the basic truth that society is an integrated nexus of units that feed into each other. The child is born. He is raised by parents. The parents are working class members of society. They must be trained for the employment that they would best fit in. As they fit into it and carry out their functions, they should earn decent wages to take care of themselves and their dependants.

Nigeria needs a top-down review. Such a review should be technical, holistic and comprehensive, and should answer a basic question such as: "Twenty years from now, where do we expect the nation to be?" This is what is called scenario planning. And no great success today can come without it.

In carrying out this exercise, we would need to take into consideration all of the statistics and then proceed to simulate the potential effects of the choices we make. For example, when we look at the factor of population in Nigeria today, two things immediately come to mind. The first is that it is one that is almost guaranteed to continue rising and the other is that it is still a very poorly skilled, poorly consuming and principally unproductive (in a competitive sense) pack.

What this then suggests is the need to create scenarios that would address this reality and threats triggered by these observations in such a way as to not only prevent negative consequences but also to more vigorously make this population an advantage for the nation and indeed the peoples of Africa and the world.

Related to the high population numbers is the shifting demographics that have now changed the total geo-spatial densities of the nation and continues to do so. Once, the bulk of Nigerians lived in rural areas. Today, we do have an essentially urban-based population. A few years ago, only a few hundred thousand people could be found in the Lagos area. Today, we are talking of 20 million and counting. And the impact of this largely unplanned growth is evident, even at the most basic level, in the very long hours that commuters spend in getting from one part of the city to the other.

Even more than time "burnt" in traffic, there are other effects. These include the quality of life of the citizens, an increasingly eroding socio-communal space and a creeping invasion of the culture of individualism that once used to be only associated with "distant societies". Urbanisation is no respecter of boundaries. Once it comes, it does so on its own terms. Thus, while it also has a bevy of benefits, the time to plan and put in measures to mitigate its ill-effect is now.

It is important here to state that urbanisation basically is not a negative phenomenon. Overall, it is connected with industrialisation, growth and development. It requires critical thinking and a commitment to shared enobling values to promote and put in place systems that would give it a human face. For example, in Lagos, enormous sums of money have been invested in the creation and support of a clean and decent environment to mitigate the ill-effects of urbanisation. There are investments in mass transit, street sweeping, parks, greening the city, etc. All of these are to help build the ambience of a more caring community and social space.

One other very fundamental challenge that the nation needs to address now is that of deliberately designing the Nigerian economy. This is because the core economic engagements we have been involved in this far have largely been imposed on us. Agriculture, our first main economic activity, was imposed on us by nature and primal need. And even today, our oil economy has only come about because we woke up to find ourselves in an eco-system that has the resource trapped under its soils and waters.

While not discountenancing these God-given assets, we need to take it a step further to the level of value addition and value creation. This is at the heart of the matter and accounts for why 50 years after Independence, we remain an import-dependent nation.

If we draw examples from China, India, Malaysia, Singapore and other nations with about the same, or even lower per capita income as Nigeria in 1960, we will discover that the basic enabling factor for their growth and linchpin for our non-growth and recession is that they added value to their resources, starting with their educational system. With value as a national attitude, they refused to settle for the distortions of leadership profligacy and citizen inertia which is very common in Nigeria today. Consequently, the entire nation has been boosted and life is better for everyone.

In almost all of these examples, they began with the basics. And here, there are two issues. One is the law of needs, so ably outlined by social researchers. And the other is the age-old wisdom bequeathed by the sages to us that any enterprise can only grow by ensuring that it gets more than it gives out. In business, for example, you only succeed by earning more than you spend.

As Maslow put it, there are basic needs that the average human has. And the first tier needs are critical, essential and compulsory. He listed them to include food, shelter and clothing. A society has only began to count very seriously when it has taken full-proof steps to ensure that it can meet these needs and in a controlled, cost-effective and non-disruptive way. Thus, the most prosperous societies in the world today are also those that have answered the issue of these needs in the most productive, sustainable and cost-effective way.

The second issue has to do with the need to ensure that the nation does not dispense of her vital foreign exchange in a way that is not value-adding. Spending foreign exchange to procure items that can be procured with local currency in Nigeria is not wisdom. It would lead to unhealthy balance of payments situation which circumscribes our capacity to attract the more significant resources that we need to grow other more needful sectors.

Indeed, this issue of currency and foreign exchange management must necessarily attract greater scrutiny going forward. As a player in the nation's financial system today, I am aware that there is a lot of avoidable movement without motion that takes place within. But the levers to be used in controlling and adjusting this situation have more often than not been put in the hands of political authorities who may not be in a hurry to do so.

But the effects are huge. Take, for example, the issue of Federation Account allocations. Given our slim tax base, the bulk of the nation's revenues today come in the form of foreign exchange payments for crude oil sales. In making allocations to component entities of the federation, this is subsequently done in naira, necessitating a conversion of such foreign earnings to naira before they are then disbursed to the entities. Given the import-dependent structure of the economy, a significant chunk of this converted foreign exchange, days after their disbursement, gets to be converted again into foreign currencies so that the nation can pay for her imports and meet other foreign exchange-denominated bills. And, of course, all of these come with charges, not to talk of the liquidity challenges that have now become systemic fare! A few economists in the past have made proposals on how this system can be adjusted in the national interest. It seems that we take this debate a lot more seriously and move to ensuring a firmer handle on our foreign exchange management platform.

The deeper tragedy of how we have carried on this far is in its implications for the future. Take the critical issues in the land today. There are insurgencies. There are fights over resource allocation and control, and disputations over the sharing of limited political offices and patronage. There is massive unemployment. But these are only super structural expositions because at the foundation, we do have an almost completely dysfunctional and largely unproductive social arrangement that does not holistically match work done with reward received in its most elementary form.

A hundred years from now, where would we be? It is clear. If we do not reform, we may almost not make it. The nation would not exist. Her peoples or the survivors of those that survive would have been far-flung and scattered. There would be issues of identity and the apocryphal title used by the visionary Chinua Achebe would very sadly have been lived out in the epitaph: There was a Country!

But we can still reverse the trend. And it will not be like re-inventing the wheel or going to the moon. What is needed is to simply appreciate that the road we are taking today is the wrong one. We should then simply stop, turn and embark on course correction. This may take and involve a number of new verities. First, the day will come soon when the depleting resource – oil – upon which we significantly depend would either be no more or would not count significantly in the global energy equation. If we remain tied to its apron strings so dependently, we would be sorry losers on that day. So, we must prepare for the reality of what is now being called, and here we paraphrase Delta State Governor Emmanuel Uduaghan, Nigeria without oil.

Second, the real wealth of the oil asset is not in the mere possession of the crude under our soil but in its extraction, refining and process improvements. And now has been added from the examples of states like Norway and Dubai, the ability to maximally yield further benefits from the oil patrimony by re-investing earned revenues in other sectors, directly or through the mechanism of a Sovereign Wealth Fund (SWF). For Nigeria to benefit better from her possession of the resource today, she has to better manage the oil asset with a view to ensuring that it yields maximum returns that are in turn maximally re-invested. In summary, rent is not enough!

Third, we need, as a matter of strategic choice, to insist on stretching the lifespan of our oil resources as much as we can. This is because even when alternatives are being developed, none comes as cheap as oil today. Equally, the transition to new technologies is also a costly venture. Why should we sell off all of our oil today and like others be forced at high costs to change all of our systems to new energy streams when it is all spent, when we can as a matter of policy begin to consciously save and retain some of our oil and, therefore, be like one of those five virgins who will yet have some oil left, when others have run out of supplies. At that time, if they must buy from us, it will be at a premium. We can now slowly, deliberately and cost-effectively, arrange for our own transition to the post-oil years without the pressures of overnight change!

Next is the issue of gas. With our huge stock of natural gas resources, we must also now begin a conscious policy of tapping more seriously our gas assets for not just foreign revenue but also to settle local industrial issues and deepen our own domestic gas economy. In this wise, we must put in place the appropriate policies to stimulate investments in gas for cars, cooking gas, heating gas and the like. The flaring of gas must end and we should move on to a new regime where gas fuels our electricity systems better and our cars and machinery more efficiently.

And then there is the issue of agriculture. As outlined earlier, food and agricultural resources are very basic to man. We must continue to drive for self sufficiency in basic food production and ensure that such food is provided for our people at affordable and not prohibitive prices. There is also another advantage of seriously investing in agriculture. It will create lots of jobs in the value chain and in this manner would be frontally addressing the scourge of unemployment which is one of the biggest demons in the land today.

And then there is the issue of education. We cannot but restate again and again the imperative of deep and functional education. In the modern world today, a people without sound and competitive education, are non-starters. The world is measured in terms of productive skills deployed into projects and activities. These are heavily driven by technology and highly improved processes and one cannot get same outside of the school system that adequately prepares the citizens for this scenario in a systematic way. In order for our educational system to deliver the goods, it must be skills-based, productive and planned.

Finally, we have to look at which of the models that can be adopted as a starting frame. The China model comes up for recommendation here. In the 1940s and 1950s, China was a large and fumbling state. Poverty was rampant, warlords lurked everywhere and the country was unable to function in a proper and structured sense. Then they began to set the critical objectives that they must meet in order to achieve sustained development. They had to feed themselves, dress themselves, grow a manufacturing base, be aggressive with exports, etc. Today, China has pushed herself so well that she is the second largest economy in the world and has become the toast of the whole world. Yesterday's problem-child has made it good in many respects.

Nigeria is not China and should not be China. But she can learn from that country's successes as well as those of others. What is critical is to recognise that our country is in a bind today and that it is the citizens who have made the conscious decision to be more nationalistic and patriotic, that would fix it. We need to freeze our long running and terminal systemic decline and begin to re-calibrate our growth in its proper frame. Therein lies the path to real sustained growth and development. Surely, it is still possible to save the future of Nigeria and create a new nation that is anchored on the visionary underpinnings of dynamic growth and sustainable socio-economic and political development. Yes, a new Nigeria is possible!

8

The Squandering of Riches: How Nigeria wasted Her Oily Opportunity to Greatness

In an address she delivered as guest speaker at the National Summit of the opposition party, the All Progressives Congress (APC) in Abuja on March 6, 2014, former Minister of Education, Oby Ezekwesili, painted a very sorry picture of the tragedy of under-development and stagnation in Nigeria contrasting the Nigerian situation with that of countries like Singapore, Malaysia, South Korea, Brazil and Chile, contemporaries with whom she began the march for development in the 1960s from about the same starting block. Ezekwesili finds very puzzling the fact that while everyone else was growing in geometric proportions, Nigeria, in a manner of speaking, has literally insisted that she did not want to be rushed!

More dramatic is that this wide gap between these nations and Nigeria was not always the case as some relevant data at the time of our independence reveal. In 1960, the GDP per capita of all these countries were not starkly different from that of Nigeria: two were below $200, two were a little above $300 and one was slightly above $500 while that of Nigeria was just about $100. For citizens, these differentials are not mere economic data. Meanwhile by 2011, the range for all five grew exponentially with Singapore at nearly $50,000, South Korea at $22,000, Malaysia at $10,000, Brazil at $13,000 and Chile at $14,000.'

Insisting that there was a clear need to interrogate the propelling factors for this *kwashiorkor* condition, the erudite public speaker proceeds to posit some questions that could help in this journey.

Our own paltry $1,500 income per capita helps drive home the point that we have been left behind many times over by every one of these other countries. How did these nations steer and stir their people to achieve such outstanding economic performance over the last five decades? There is hardly a basis for comparing the larger population of our citizens clustered within the poverty bracket with the majority citizens of Singapore fortunate to have upper middle income standard of living.

Again, how did this happen? What happened to Nigeria? Why did we get left behind? How did these nations become productively wealthy over the last fifty three years while Nigeria stagnated? How did majority of the citizens of these nations join the upper middle class while more Nigerians retrogressed into poverty? There are usually as many different answers to these sets of questions as there are respondents on the reasons we fell terribly behind.

Reviewing relevant literature on the subject, Ezekwesili next goes on to contradict some of the clearly aberrant ration-alisations that have since emerged in the debate.

Some say, it is our tropical geography, yet economic research shows it has not prevented other countries like China, Australia, Chile and Brazil for example with similar conditions from breaking through economically. Others say it is size, but China and India are bigger, and yet in the last thirty and twenty years have grown double digit and continue to out-grow the rest of the world at this time of global economic crisis. Furthermore, being small has not necessarily conferred any special advantages to so many other countries with small population yet similarly battling with the development process like we are.

Some others say it is our culture but like a political economist posited "European countries with different sorts of cultures, Protestant and Catholic alike that have grown rich. Secondly, different countries within the same broad cultures have performed very differently in economic terms, such as the two Koreas in the post-war era. Moreover, individual countries have changed their economic trajectories even though "their cultures didn't miraculously change".

How about those who plead our multi ethnic nationalities as the constraint but fail to see that the United States of America happens to be one nation with even more disparate ethnic nationalities than Nigeria and yet it leads the global economy! As for those who say it is the adverse impact of colonialism, were Singapore, Malaysia and even parts of China like Hong Kong not similarly conquered and dominated by colonialists?

Even more painful in all of this is the sheer impact that this scenario has had on the majority of the Nigerian people and the composite image of the nation. Hear her:

That Nigeria is a paradox of the kind of wealth that breeds penury is as widely known as the fact that the world considers us a poster nation for poor governance wealth from natural resources. The trend of Nigeria's population in poverty since 1980 to 2010 for example suggests that the more we earned from oil, the larger the population of poor citizens:17.1 million 1980, 34.5million in 1985, 39.2million in 1992, 67.1million in 1996, 68.7million in 2004 and 112.47 million in 2010! This sadly means that you are children of a nation blessed with abundance of ironies.

Resource wealth has tragically reduced your nation – my nation – to a mere parable of prodigality.

Nothing undignifies nations and their citizens like self-inflicted failure. Our abundance of oil, people and geography should have worked favorably and placed us on the top echelons of the global economic ladder by now. After all, basic economic evidence shows that abundance of natural resources can by itself increase the income levels of citizens even if it does not increase their productivity. For example, as Professor Collier a renowned economist who has focused on the sector stated in a recent academic work countries that have enormously valuable natural resources are likely to have high living standards on a sustainable basis by simply replacing some of the extracted resources with financial assets held abroad. Disappointedly, even that choice eluded our governing class who through the decades has spent more time quarrelling over their share of the oil "national cake" than they have spent thinking of how to make it benefit the entire populace.

The coup of 1966 anchored its justification on the failure of the political class to provide good governance. In the exact words of the leader of the coup;

> Our enemies are the political profiteers, the swindlers, the men in high and low places that seek bribes and demand 10 percent; those that seek to keep the country divided permanently so that they can remain in office as ministers or VIPs at least, the tribalists, the nepotists, those that make the country look big for nothing before international circles, those that have corrupted our society and put the Nigerian political calendar back by their words and deeds.

In effect, what we today confront as systemic corruption only metamorphosed to gigantic proportion through the over nearly five decades of the speech given to justify the first truncation of the will of the people for democratic governance. As a matter of fact, anyone who will find and read all the justification statements for coups and the inauguration statements for democratically elected governments in our fifty three years of being a country will assume that each group merely modified the speech of their predecessors.

Perhaps the only differences were the locations of the punctuation marks, the commas, the semi colons and the full stops in each statement that followed this excerpt from the statement of 1966.

On the twin enemies of corruption and poverty, those among us who still need proof to believe that indeed the two severest maladies from which Nigeria must heal are poverty and poor governance must not have seen the 2013 Global Corruption Barometer 2013. Poverty and corruption are two things that rob Nigerians of their dignity; Poverty deprives one of the basic services they need in order to preserve their self-dignity. Poor governance on the other hand is what poverty helps breed.

Thus, academic research shows that countries which have tended to poor governance end delivering not delivering the basic social services that citizens need in order to lift themselves out of poverty and where they do at all, it is too little and too poor a quality to make a difference. It is the capacity to constantly deliver equality of opportunities for better quality of life to all citizens that distinguishes one government from another.

Throughout our fifty-three year history following our independence in 1960, we sadly have not recorded one stellar record of performance in this regard by any government. Today, our 69% poor in the land which in real number terms translates to over 100 million citizens trapped in poverty.

Specifically on the place of petroleum earnings in the economy, she would not be restrained:

Take the natural resources sector to which we have willingly and disastrously mortgaged our lives to as a result of failure of leadership to embrace hard work, effort and productivity as national values. Nigeria is Africa's largest oil exporter, and the world's 10th largest oil producer, accounting for more than 2.2 million barrels a day in 2011. Oil revenues totaled $50.3 billion in 2011 and generated more than 70 percent of government revenues. However, for a sector that sadly determines our rise and fall in the last fifty three years, Nigeria's Performance on the Resource Governance Index (carried out by the global NGO- Revenue Watch Institute of the Open Society Foundations) – Nigeria received a "weak" score of 42, ranking 40th out of 58 countries.

We stood out among the 80% of countries which fail to achieve good governance in their extractive sectors. The insalubrious performance of this dominant revenue source seems to be one we have decided to wear elegantly with a mindset that refuses to embrace the kind of fundamental change that will set the nation free. A read of the now famous in the breach, PIB shows that we have refused to surrender and subordinate the huge power of discretion exercised by the President in all matters concerning oil since the last many decades. Surely, for what we know of the huge benefits of transparency and competition it does indeed stir the minds of those that have no interest in oil blocks but who care for the maximization of value for the aggregate social good of Nigeria that we walk the provisions of our NEITI law.

The pervasive hold over our economy by oil shows up in everything. In our Sovereign credit rating recently, poor governance, low per capita Gross Domestic Product (GDP) and reserve cover were identified as Nigeria's biggest challenge to joining other Emerging Markets (EMs) according to Richard Fox of Fitch Ratings. According to him, these areas represent Nigeria's biggest challenge to improving its rating, as highlighted in Fitch's previous research.

Of the three, reserve cover is the most susceptible to rapid improvement, particularly at current high oil prices. This is because although at that time of his comment, Nigeria's reserves had risen by around $2 billion they are not rising as fast as in the majority of big oil exporters". Comparisons always help convey these kinds of information better.

During the period, 2009 to 2011 Algeria expanded her savings from current oil boom by at least 30% to build up its reserve and invest in critical infrastructure. The new comer Angola nearly doubled its reserve while simultaneously implementing a huge public investment program to build diversity of critical infrastructure.

Sadly, whether it is building up reserves/saving or in building critical infrastructure and human capital our own trend is in the reverse. For even though crude price rose or has held steady at different time, the quality of governance continues to hobble our capacity to strike out onto the path of success.

To underscore the colossal weight of the tragedy in which the country has fallen, Ezehwesili draws on even other examples and makes stunning comparisons.

> It cost $148bn dollars in today's value to rebuild Europe after the World War II. This is less than half of the funds that was attributed to have been stolen from Nigeria since independence. The expense of such funds transformed the manufacturing, service industry and competitive factors of Europe. It cost $2bn ($349bn in today's value) to rebuild Japan after the nuclear attack.

> By conservative estimate, our country has earned more than $600billion in the last five decades and yet can only boast of a United Nations Human Development Index score of .4 out of 1 proximate to that of Chad and maternal mortality rate similar to that of Afghanistan! Nothing reveals the depth of our failures than such performance indicators considering the vastly greater possibilities that we have been bestowed.

And then she closes with a hopeful ring that even as this atrophy set in for Nigeria, there was equally emerging the beginning of the corresponding rise of a critical mass that she believes the future of the nation can be safely entrusted:

> Citizens now seek to fully participate and make demands for democratic accountability- they are not afraid to scrutinise all public institutions and to demand better results of governance. The unwillingness of any group of political elite to understand this emerging power of the Office of the Citizen can only be a loss to the former and yet another missed opportunity added to our-canvass of political tragedies....... But God forbid!

Dr. Ezekwesili may be faulted for blowing hot and cold, but we have decided to copiously explore the core points of her presentation because there is a sense in which it strikes at the heart of the matter. Indeed, despite what many think and feel, the path of success is not really that mysterious. Very simply, it consists of a few steps that if taken would lead the seeker there. And if you do not take those steps, your destination is equally guaranteed: a place that is not SUCCESS.

While it will take more than a few swipes at the keyboard to outline all of the principles of success, suffice it to say that some of the more essential variables that make for success are indeed quite discernible. The one that must succeed at something must as a matter of primal necessity first have a supervening vision of what he wants. He must also research and think through his envisioned goal thoroughly, preferably write it down, outline its key processes, give it numbers, count the costs and make a strong and unwavering commitment to this stated goal and purpose (the ancient Hebrews will demand a formal covenant).

Next, he must get onto his feet and begin to gather in all of the ingredients that would be required for the task at hand. These would include specific knowledge on how to proceed, the precise steps to be taken, the funding, technical inputs and expertise, personnel, management and quality definition, and control. And after this gathering phase, he must very diligently and sacrificially get to work on the project and remain at it no matter how the wind blows. This is how success happens for men; it is also how it is with nations. When these steps are not taken, success is no longer guaranteed. And for Nigeria, our story begins at Oloibiri.

Early Beginnings

A contemporary visitor to Oloibiri in Bayelsa State, Nigeria, will ask the question: is this really the place? The community looks disused, infrastructure is maximally absent and you can see very obviously that the community does not have any of the splendour you will find in upscale Lagos, the Federal Capital Territory, Abuja, or even neighbouring Port Harcourt. Things are that bad and Oloibiri is

Nigeria's primal metaphor of what that most perceptive philosopher described as "the road not taken".

Nigeria's rise to join the league of oil producers was indeed an epochal one. For a journey that formally started in 1938 when prospectors first commenced exploratory search for crude oil within the territory of Nigeria, and this was in the season following the formal amalgamation of the Southern and Northern Protectorates of Nigeria; events both within the nation as well as global occurrences and factors were to play themselves out in this journey. Some of these included the early steps in establishing British colonial overlordship over what was going to become perhaps its most ambitious colonial project in Africa, the entrenchment of the overhanging British imperial strategy to essentially relate to Nigeria as a trading, cash crop and mining economy, the outbreak of the two world wars and the subsequent agitation for the decolonisation of the territory and continent.

For several years now, the debate over the full intentions of direct British colonial occupation in Nigeria has tended to insinuate that Britain was largely in the dark as to the oil-bearing potentials of her most populous African colony. For proponents of this view, they argue that since economics was a central factor in the determination of Britain to annex the Nigerian protectorates in the first place, and even to hold on further to her then prized East African colony, Kenya, a similar decision would have been taken in respect of not disengaging from Nigeria without the equivalent of a "bloody fight", had Britain had the full picture of how much "black gold" truly lay underneath the soils and waters of the West African behemoth over which she had established full and formal sovereignty.

But the facts, however, point in another direction. As documents from the colonial archives bear out, British interest in Nigerian oil originated in the year of amalgamation, 1914, with the gazetting of an ordinance making any oil and mineral under Nigerian soil legal property of the Crown. Indeed, it was on the strength of this law that the colonial government in 1938 acceded to a commercial request from the state-sponsored company, Shell (then known as

Shell D'Arcy) and granted her monopoly status over the exploration of all minerals and petroleum throughout the entire colony.

Though the company commenced operations almost immediately, it was, however, not until 1958 that commercially viable oil was to be discovered by Shell roughly 90 km west of the soon-to-be oil capital of Port Harcourt at Oloibiri (now in Bayelsa State). And in an early indication of what was later to develop into the "Joint Venture" (JV) practice which is still the economic fulcrum for many of the investments by prospecting firms in the nation's oil industry, the initial business structure of this partnership was a 50-50 profit sharing system between the company and the colonial government.

Right into the late 1950s, all concessions on production and exploration of oil in the territory and nation of Nigeria continued to be the exclusive domain of Shell, which was then known as the Shell-British Petroleum. However, other firms soon became interested and by the early 1960s, Mobil, Texaco, and Gulf had let themselves into the action through purchasing concessions and commencing independent exploration forays within the country.

This flurry of activities notwithstanding, the historic commencement of drilling operations by Shell itself was, however, not a most remarkable champagne event for the British Crown, its colonial government in Nigeria and the core of the indigenous political leadership that had by now begun to take over the rungs of government. Part of the reason for this may have been the fact that it had taken two decades of patient but wearying investment and work to get there. A second reason may have been the absence of very reliable data then to correctly provide estimates of the potential volume of oil that was available within the pioneering drilling acreages as well as the prospects for finding more. The third reason is the issue of British honour, given that since the beginning of the decade of the 1950s, Her Majesty's Government had actually commenced a slow but deliberate programme of colonial disengagement which the Crown was sure to lose face over should it decide to abort it then. And fourth, the "lukewarm" response from the new Nigerian political leaders would be attributed to some of the factors above, but also to the fact that given the nature of the federal constitution that was then in place, the new resources were largely going to concern the specific region from where the find had been made, namely, the Eastern Region.

There was another issue: oil, as it were, was a new element in the national economic mix and it clearly had not come to occupy the pride of place that it has presently assumed.

But with many in the world and indeed in the soon-to-be-independent colony yet oblivious of the new-found wealth that was available to Nigeria, there were some that were already becoming aware of this. And as the young nation took her first steps down the path of freedom, some of these issues began to come to the fore.

The first was in the same year of discovery, 1958, when, between the British colonial administrators, the leaders of the oil-bearing Niger-Delta region and the rest of the nationalist leaders who had been engaged in talks about the future structure and shape of the soon-to-be-independent nation, a Willinks Commission was empanelled to look into the "Special Needs" of the oil-bearing areas. That report which made a strong case for special environmental protection and commensurate development of the area was to be added to the resultant Independence Constitution.

Indeed, it is in protest over the perceived neglect of these "Special Needs" that the late policeman, Isaac Adaka Boro, proceeded to establish a rebel army that took to the creeks in an attempt to wage war against Nigeria. Though that insurrection failed, it clearly was one of the most significant fuels for the activities of latter-day bands of Niger-Delta militants, some of whom are presently undergoing rehabilitation and re-integration into the larger Nigerian society as we write.

There has also been a debate as to how much the nation's new-found oil discovery – and her colossal prospects for wealth acquisition by anyone who had control over the territory under which she lay – contributed to the Nigerian civil war. However, there is no argument that the oil companies knew what indeed was at stake, and that very likely through them, other frontline actors in the fray, the critical world powers then, the bands of mercenaries, were ultimately to be brought to speed on the reality that the core theatre of the conflict was equally a seat of colossal wealth.

Rising Awareness

As things developed then, the progression of the war saw a corresponding increase not only of the production volume of crude oil drilled from within the country but also in Nigerian oil literacy and general awareness about the new source of wealth in the nation and its potential to soon become a net revenue earner for the country. Decisions, alliances, payments, MoUs, IOUs, and other critical levers of political, military and economic power as they had to do with the nation and the prosecution of the war effort increasingly came to depend on the inflow of oil revenues and an overall appreciation of the "oil factor".

For the nation overall, however, it was to take a decade post-Oloibiri for oil revenues to begin to make a fairly significant dot on the nation's income profile. And because there was a corresponding element of power play and denial involved, as well as the absence of a very clear programme on how to respond to the new bumper revenues that were falling into the laps of the ill-prepared generals and manipulating civil servants that were at that time holding the reins of government, it came at a huge cost to the nation and her people.

The importance of a well-defined programme of growth and development for any people is very important. In Singapore, for instance, Lee Kuan Yew and his band of reformers followed hard upon this path and the result is the astounding story of spectacular growth and development that continues to inspire many in the world today.

As is evident in the Singapore story and in many others the world over, one of the first ingredients for success is a visionary leader. Nigeria, in the very critical post-Independence years, had a vast range of issues going against her such that it was very difficult for the young nation to crystallise the type of leadership impetus that was needed at this most critical time. As if this was not enough, the dwarfish and Lilliputian leaders that situations, conflicts and circumstances had thrown up now had the added burden of finding themselves awash in great oil wealth and with no discernible plan on what to do with it! The resource had become a curse!

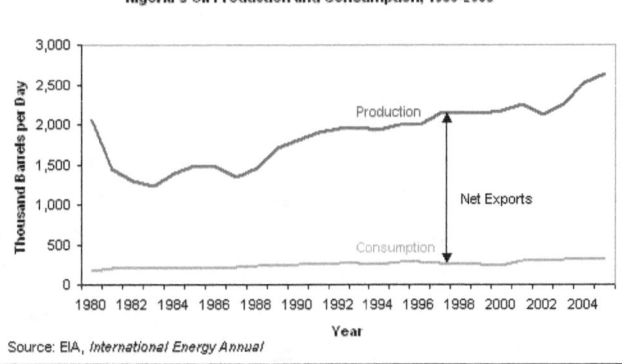

Nigeria's Oil Production and Consumption, 1980-2005

Source: EIA, *International Energy Annual*

Many dictionaries describe squandering as relating to the act of spending resources in a wasteful manner. With very poor leadership at the fore, Nigeria's oil wealth has, therefore, been squandered in a number of ways, as shown below:

1. The emphasis on the primary production of crude oil has cost the country potential wealth that would have accrued from the concomitant exploitation of the secondary and tertiary crude oil processing applications in the form of value-added sales revenues, skilled indigenous manpower and a developed petrochemical complex complete with spin-off petrochemical and allied industries. What clearly would have been a peg for the sure industrialisation of the nation and a channel for establishing the country as a foremost player in the global petrochemical and extended industrial complex has come to be a poverty-spinner and de-industrialising linchpin.

2. The poor deployment of oil revenues in recurrent and capital expenditure projects in successive national budgets. Overall, the nation's oil revenues have been treated as "harvest" to be

shared and not "seed" to be re-invested, leading to economic *kwashiorkor*, with the nation producing a wealthy few in the midst of a vastly impoverished people and the equally aberrant situation where the national budgetary cycle has come to be an annual corruption-laden rush to empty the treasuries before the next tranche of oil revenues come in which would in turn also be hastily emptied in a vicious cycle that leaves the entire nation and her people infinitely poorer.

3. The shift of emphasis from agriculture and other productive streams. Unlike in the past where a more pragmatic planning framework was in place leading to the nation generating sustainable and trickle-back income from agriculture, agro-allied and the then better-regulated mining industries, the current crude oil export-dominated economy is largely built upon a very denuding framework where the real sector is vastly alienated and well over 90 percent of the total economic value that ought to be available to all is in the hands of a few well-connected power-mongers and their allies.

4. The encouragement and uplifting of the negative vices of graft and laziness to the status of national culture which has bred a generation of carpet-baggers or people who are constantly plotting on how to get access to the "freely floating" oil wealth and not productive life-long careers and occupations.

5. The lowering of the psyche of the average Nigerian. Contrast the average citizen today who is hungry and desperate to emigrate "to just anywhere but this country" with the response of the economically assured Okonkwo in Chinua Achebe's *Things Fall Apart* who very sorely laments his temporary banishment from Umuofia to Mbanta on account of a grievous homicide and you will see how low the psyche of the Nigerian has sunk.

Comparative Analysis

A critical appraisal of the immense revenue accruing from Nigeria's oil wealth and its frittering has demonstrated that unlike other similarly endowed nations, the country has virtually wasted a chance of a lifetime.

United Arab Emirates

Take the United Arab Emirates, for example. When the Gulf nation discovered crude oil in commercial quantity, her rulers who had long been weaned on a diet of almost permanent lack on account of the country's arid desert location, wisely decided to deploy the newfound wealth in the manner of seeds. They looked out for new and sustainable growth areas and decided to invest in them as a way of ensuring the longevity of her resource-base. The Dubai Media City, complete with its myriad of enterprises and commercial endeavours, is an epigrammatic lesson for all today.

Interestingly, in the Dubai story can also be found an apocryphal tale relating to Nigeria and the parable of the road not taken. As the tale goes, in the years preceding Dubai's discovery of oil and when a Nigerian head of state had loudly boasted that Nigeria's problem was not money but how to spend it, the rulers of the pre-oil Dubai, who had been going round cap in hand looking for more endowed nations that would come to her aid had sent a powerful delegation to Nigeria on a mission to get the West African nation to invest in some of their development projects

After listening to the delegation, the then head of state had sent a fact-finding mission to Dubai with a view to conducting due diligence on the presentation by the Dubai team. The mission went, saw and returned with a No: "the place was all desert and sand and there was no prospect that the project could thrive and prosper!" The rest, as they say, is history. The Dubai project has since been established and continues to thrive even as it has also discovered the same crude oil which had brought it this way in the first place.

Norway Also

A second example of a nation that found oil and very wisely decided not to fritter away the concomitant wealth that it brought would be the Scandinavian nation of Norway. At the close of last year, all Norwegians become crown millionaires, in an oil saving landmark that epitomises the difference between oil producing nations for which the resource has come to be metaphorically equated as being a curse and others for whom the resource is widely acknowledged to be a blessing.

According to a report by the news agency, Reuters, the elevation of all Norwegians to the status of theoretical crown millionaire was indeed a milestone for the world's biggest sovereign wealth fund (SWF) whose revenues literally ballooned thanks to a combination of high oil and gas prices and deft management of the resulting fortunes.

Set up in 1990, the Norwegian SWF owns around 1 percent of the world's stocks, as well as bonds and real estate from London to Boston, making the Nordic nation an exception in the world today even as other nations, including fellow oil producers like Nigeria, are struggling under a mountain of under-development, resource misapplication and debts.

A preliminary counter on the website of the central bank, which manages the fund, rose to 5.11 trillion crowns ($828.66 billion), fractionally more than a million times Norway's most recent official population estimate of 5,096,300. It was indeed the first time it reached the equivalent of a million crowns each.

Not that Norwegians will be able to access or spend the money, squirreled away for a rainy day for them and future generations. Norway has resisted the temptation to splurge the entire windfall since striking oil in the North Sea in 1969; precisely one decade after Nigeria had received her own windfall at Oloibiri in 1958. The Finance Minister Siv Jensen told Reuters that above any other thing, the Fund, which is specifically denoted as the Government Pension Fund Global, had helped iron out big, unpredictable swings in oil and gas prices for the number seven oil exporter in the world.

Underscoring that the essence of the entire investment schedule was simply and squarely to put away something in anticipation of a day in the future when both the flow of income and place of oil as a leading resource earner for the small nation of historically hard-working, forward-looking and diligent citizens would no longer be assured, Jensen lamented the very puzzling fact that "many countries have found that temporary large revenues from natural resource exploitation produce relatively short-lived booms that are followed by difficult adjustments".

He did not have to call Nigeria by name as being a prime and most fitting example under reference. As an Igbo proverb made popular by the eminent novelist, Chinua Achebe, in *Things Fall Apart*, would say, an old woman surely gets uneasy when dry bones are mentioned in a proverb.

Even more than its paper value, are the deeper growth implications of Norway's SWF. In real value terms, the Fund was equivalent to 183 percent of Norway's 2013 gross domestic product, is expected to peak at 220 percent around 2030. And before proceeding any further, it has to be noted also that Norway's GDP is, and has continued to rank as one of the highest in the world in the past two decades.

Commentators on the Norwegian success story have, like the minister, been equally enthused. "The fund is a success in the sense that parliament has managed to put aside money for the future. There are many examples of countries that have not managed that," says Oeystein Doerum, chief economist at DNB Markets.

Part of the success of the framework is that Norway *ab initio* took a conscious decision to avoid the boom and burst cycle that is synonymous with economies that become too liquid on account of their colossal earnings by investing the cash abroad, rather than at home. And the specific governance framework in place is that governments can spend 4 percent of the Fund in Norway each year, slightly more than the annual return on investment.

Still, in Norway, oil wealth may have made the state reluctant to make reforms or cut subsidies unthinkable elsewhere. Farm subsidies allow farmers, for instance, to keep dairy cows in heated barns in the Arctic! On the flip side, it may also have made some Norwegians reluctant to work. "One in five people of working age receives some kind of social insurance instead of working," Doerum says, despite an official unemployment rate of 3.3 percent.

But if Norway is having "attitude problems" on account of her wealth as a nation, the situation in less disciplined nations like Nigeria is indeed gargantuan. In May 2013, a report that tracked resource mismanagement and corruption in 58 countries, indicted successive governments in Nigeria for not meeting "satisfactory standards" for managing the country's enormous oil wealth and natural resources.

The report, Resource Governance Index, released by New York-based Revenue Watch Institute (RWI), according to Reuters, said over 80 percent of the world's major oil and gas-producing and mining countries failed the resource management and corruption test. The Index ranked Nigeria, which produces and exports an average of two million barrels of oil per day, as example, whose oil revenues were 60 percent more than total international aid to sub-Saharan Africa in 2011, very high in resource mismanagement and corruption.

According to Reuters, the RWI noted that should the Nigerian governments and others improve the way they manage these resources, it would make a significant difference in their economic development. "The lives of over a billion citizens could be transformed if their governments managed their oil, gas and minerals in a more open, accountable manner," Revenue Watch reported.

The Index, which is released annually, is designed to help commodity-rich countries avoid the so-called "resource curse", in which their economies grow only slowly due to poor institutional oversight.

The Revenue Watch findings are not totally novel. When she returned to Nigeria after her sojourn in the United States, Onyeka Owenu, the artist and media worker, made a film on the subject of Nigeria's oil blitz. Entitled, "Nigeria: A Squandering of Riches", the film outlined in very graphic details how the citizens of the nation were wallowing in abject poverty even in the midst of plenty. In a 2008 piece in *Tell* magazine, Lucas Ajanaku continues on this theme, asserting that Nigeria's oil wealth has not translated into meaningful development largely due to bad leadership and corruption. In the report, he relived a presentation by Antonio Maria Costa, the Executive Director at the United Nations Office on Drug and Crime (UNODC), who spoke at a national seminar organised by the Economic and Financial Crimes Commission (EFCC), in Abuja.

As Maria Costa spoke, most of his audience literally paled cold. According to him, between 1960 when Nigeria became independent and 1999 when democracy was restored, a staggering sum of $400 billion was stolen and stashed away by a generation of corrupt rulers. That is within a space of 39 years. And the discovery of oil, the nation's cash cow, predates independence. "If you were to put $400 billion bills in a row, you could make a path from here to the moon and back not once but 75 times. The opportunity cost of the stolen common wealth is enormous. Think of how different Nigeria would (have) looked today," Maria Costa lamented.

Underscoring Costa's revelation, the same report under reference draws allusions to the submissions of the maverick Tam David-West, a long-standing professor of Virology at the University of Ibadan, son of the Niger-Delta and one-time oil minister in the country. Recalls David West: "Shell BP began by exporting 5,100 barrels per day, bpd, in 1958." And to confirm that there was indeed a lot from where that first consignment came, in 1959, production output literally jumped to about 10,000 bpd! Of course, production and export figures have since continued to rise exponentially almost year-on-year until the current time when it has attained about 2.4 million bpd, and in the process translating into some of the astounding financial resources, the abuse of which continues to confound people everywhere. "That is a lot of money. But, where is the money? There is nothing to show for it," says David-West as he equally joins the lamentation party.

Another respondent, Frank Kokori, frontline trade unionist and veteran of many battles to properly position Nigerian workers within the petroleum sector, says that the advent of oil in Nigeria marked an unfortunate turning point in the nation's history as it led to the emergence of a crop of lazy citizens who lost the initiative to be productive. According to Kokori, the country became a dumping ground for imported goods as cheap dollars flowed ceaselessly from petroleum. "The sad commentary about the Nigerian situation is that it is one of the few countries that pump out more than two million bpd and still live in this primitive infrastructural situation. Oil boom has become oil doom," he said.

In his own comment, Tunji Otegbeye, labour leader, Zikist nationalist and elder statesman, traced the beginning of the woes of the nation to the doorsteps of the military. "The military merely captured the economy, and looting was at its best at that time. There is no doubt that the military ruined the economy of this country from the beginning to the end. There is also the chop-chop machinery of the politicians to contend with. And so, Nigeria has gone from frying pan into fire," Otegbeye said. He may be right.

The most brazen pillaging of the national economy which was lubricated by oil wealth allegedly took place under the military. Maria Costa said the late Sani Abacha, former head of state, cornered between two and three percent of the nation's GDP every year he was head of state. Perhaps, to underpin the fact that corruption was one of the legacies British colonialism bequeathed to the nation, Nzeogwu's Supreme Council of Revolution pointed at stamping out corruption as one of the reasons for sacking the Tafawa Balewa-led government. "Our enemies are the political profiteers, swindlers: those that have corrupted our society and put the Nigerian calendar back by their words and deeds," he declared in January 15, 1966.

David-West blames the nation's economic woes on the way the oil sector is run. He accused the government of Babangida of glorifying corruption, arguing that no other member-country of the Organisation of Petroleum Exporting Countries (OPEC), runs her oil industry as it is run in Nigeria. While President Babangida government "liberalised crude oil lifting process" for selfish interest, he allegedly colluded with the late Abdulkadir Ahmed, former governor of the Central Bank of Nigeria, to operate a "dedicated account" into which huge sums of money was lodged, spent and unaccounted for till date. The

$12.5 billion Gulf War oil windfall took wings and flew away without any trace. According to David-West,

> Before Babangida came, there were strict conditions for selling Nigeria's crude oil. Oil was sold to end-users and not to those who sell at Rotterdam but those with refineries that will refine the crude oil. If you do not have a refinery, you must show legal evidence that you have had oil refining contract for more than 10 years and deposit three consecutive audited reports that must show fantastic turnover and net worth. Staff strength must not be less than 20. Then oil must not be sold to South Africa because of apartheid,

David-West further laments that all these guidelines were thrown overboard when Babangida took over and crude oil was then "sold like groundnut or palm oil". Bad as that "liberalization" was, David-West laments that subsequent governments have retained it because of the lure of lucre: "They have tasted the forbidden fruit, it is sweet. The system dug a cesspit of corruption, with personal interest now taking precedent over national interest," he said.

The Real Losers

The inability of Nigeria to properly harness her crude oil earnings has continued to have massive negative impacts on the nation, her people and the immediate oil producing communities. One of the real difficulties that people and nations face is an inability to properly and effectively chart a path of vision and development. One Nigerian leader who epitomises this is General Yakubu Gowon. At the peak of his tenure as head of state in the mid-1970s, and with the treasury awash in oil wealth, Gowon had literally led the nation on a spending binge that fell short of what a more determinedly futuristic leader would have done. Privately, he was involved in organising the biggest wedding ceremony that the land had known, and publicly, he was equally driving as if his problem was how to finish the resources that were pouring in. With scant planning, he embarked on rushed development projects that led to a cement armada that needed the constitution of a task force and payment of huge demurrage fines. He became big brother, who was paying salaries of public sector workers in distant countries that asked for it! He approved the Udoji awards that led to the rapid ballooning of the middle class and the continuing scourge of a recurrent expenditure-dominated budgetary process from which the nation has been unable to recover till date. Other military and civilian leaders followed suit and the nation has continued to suffer for it.

Returning to the depths of this decay, there were also spin-offs. As rural farmers saw the stupendous increase in the earnings of civil servants and the urban elite, they were converted. They dropped their hoes and headed for the cities. This led to corresponding pressure on city infrastructure and a spike in crime rates given the reality that many of the newcomers had not fully considered how they would live productively in their new abodes. They merely tapped on the extended African family system which ensured that they would find almost handy temporary lodgings as soon as they could make it into the city. If it was not a close relative or kinsman, it would be an extended communal or linguistic relative. We are Africans!

There were equally deeper issues. The abandonment of the farm economy led to a reversal in GDP terms. Unlike in the past when the quantum of agriculture's contribution to the GDP of the nation was a handsome 80 percent, now agricultural GDP was below 50 percent.

Even more critically was the fact that there was no thorough-going effort to strongly ensure that the new GDP contributors were, in the long term, sustainable and maximally contributing to the economic base. Some of the projects were indeed ill-thought and not protected. One government bought many of the same ship. When changes in the economy and technology made that type of ship unattractive, the whole fleet had to be sold off for a pittance. Another government set up refineries across the country that have continued to under-perform, leading to the current situation where the country continues to massively import petroleum products that it could have very easily refined.

There was also a very strong disconnect between economic objectives and political goals. When the Americans moved in Gulf War 1 to rescue Kuwait from Iraqi occupation, it was not for nothing. At the close of the war, the US Government turned in an invoice for the job which the Kuwaitis paid, and for interest, it ensured that American firms got about all of the major clean-up and reconstruction contracts that were awarded!

In the instance of Nigeria, a strong focus on Africa as the centre-piece of Nigerian foreign policy for decades has not been followed with a roadmap for solid pan-African economic cooperation and synergy. Take, for example, the instance of the pan-regional grouping, the Economic Community of West African States (ECOWAS). Nigeria provides about 80 percent of the budget of ECOWAS, the principal facilitating agency for the integration of the sub-region. But it is a laggard in terms of the nations that get the highest benefits from the ECOWAS project. This is evident in the sports arena, where the sports grouping, the West African Football Union is dominated by member-states from the Francophone bloc. In the critical area of banking, though Nigeria was a major pillar in the formation of the regional banking behemoth, Ecobank, however, since the bank was conceived, its headquarters has been located in Lome, Togo, and even when today about 50 percent of the Bank's business and revenue comes from Nigeria, the affairs of that institution and indeed the immediate benefits of its existence in the form of jobs, CSR projects, etc, remain heavily skewed in favour of the Togolese and their Francophone African neighbours.

Equally problematic is the fact that the absence of an overarching economic policy for the continent has continued to leave Nigeria with the short end of the stick in relation to even economic competition from other global power centres for the consolidated African market. Travelling from Nigeria to Benin Republic, Togo, Ghana, and Cote d'Ivoire and beyond, one would find that it is the Nigerian belt that is most hostile to intra-African business cooperation. With not less than 20 road checks between Mile 2 and Seme and bad and pot-holed roads, many Nigerian businesses are not seriously encouraged to venture afield into the one billion strong African markets.

Even at the policy level, Nigeria has continued to shirk its responsibilities in the area of promoting a very strong regional currency. These are some of the things that God gave the country her vast oil resources for. It is, therefore, unfortunate that this blessing has today become a curse on account of inept, under-performing and visionless leadership. The book of Proverbs in the Bible puts it in strong terms: "Woe unto the city whose king is a child and its princes feast in the morning." How apt!

The truth about global economic development is that one generation has to sacrifice for the next. The biblical Abraham sacrificed for Isaac. The post-war Germans sacrificed for the prosperity that future generations have continued to enjoy. Ditto the post-war Japanese. The current generation of Norwegians is doing the same even today. As the generation of Gowon and Udoji were feasting even then, they were frittering away the seeds that were expected to produce the prosperity of today. We, therefore, now need a new generation of sacrificially imbued leaders that will begin to take us back to where we had missed it so we can truly begin again.

All things considered then, Gowon's economic management and that of successive bands of leaders was clearly not the way to go for a nation desiring to grow solid economic foundations.

Industry Nationalisation

Some of the definitive structural systems in the Nigerian oil sector came in the years following the close of the civil war. Shortly after the end of the civil war, and precisely in May 1971, government nationalised the oil industry by creating the Nigeria National Oil Corporation (NNOC) via a decree. This step, the government felt, was necessary to secure and gain more control over the oil industry which had, during the civil war era, not been very coordinately managed. The move to nationalise the oil sector was also informed by Nigeria's desire to join that omnibus cartel of oil producers, the Organisation of Petroleum Exporting Countries (OPEC), which required that member-states acquire at least 51 percent stake in the ownership of the central coordinating petroleum agency in member-countries and become increasingly involved in the oil sector. Although the Nigerian government had maintained a basic involvement in the industry prior to 1971, this was accomplished mainly through business deals on concessions of the foreign firms in operation. The creation of the Nigeria National Oil Company (NNOC) made government participation in the industry legally binding. Even more fortuitously, the federal government would continue to consolidate its oil involvement throughout the next several decades and even running to the present time when the composition and operations of the central government agency involved in the petroleum sector, the Nigeria National Petroleum Corporation, has become a kind of national albatross.

Stimulus Denied

The implications of the failure of Nigeria to properly grow her oil industry are legion. First, the country cannot get the bulk of the revenues ordinarily expected to be grossed by it. Second, some of the jobs and developmental opportunities that it would have provided would not be found. And third, there would be a stifling of the technological processes that the proper exploitation of the sector would have introduced.

But even more importantly is the big picture failure. Oil, being a stimulus economic product, the non-cultivation of it in proper and exhaustive forms automatically introduces a failing in the overall economic cycle: it would not be stimulated and thus would not grow.

However, it was during the years of Gowon and his successors, Murtala Mohammed and Olusegun Obasanjo, known officially as the heads of the Federal Military Government of Nigeria, who ruled amidst the oil boom of the 1970s that the political economy of petroleum in Nigeria truly became characterised by endemic patronage and corruption by the political elites, which plagues the nation to this day. At both state and federal government levels, power and, therefore, wealth have typically been monopolised by select lobby groups who maintain a strong tendency to "look after their own" by financially rewarding their political supporters. At the state or community level, this means that interest groups in power will reward and protect their own; this is typically based on ethnic/tribal or religious affiliation of the interest group. The heavy patronage based on tribal affiliation has fuelled ethnic unrest and violence throughout Nigeria, but particularly in the Niger Delta states where the stakes for control of the immense oil resources are very high. At the federal level, political elites have utilised patronage to consolidate power for the ruling government, not only by rewarding their political friends in the federal government, but also by paying off major interest groups at the state or tribal level in order to elicit their cooperation. Inevitably, these financial favours are distributed unequally and inefficiently, resulting in concentration of wealth and power in the hands of a small minority. Nigeria is in fact ranked very poorly in the Corruption Perception Index, standing at a dismal 121st, out of 180 countries surveyed, and is now one of sub-Saharan Africa's most corrupt states.

Following the NNOC's genesis, the Nigerian government persisted in garnering control over oil revenues. In 1972, it declared that all property not currently owned by a foreign entity was legally the property of the government, which gained jurisdiction of the sale and allocation of concessions to foreign investment. The military regime oversaw the implementation of a number of other important milestones related to oil:

1. 1974: Participation in oil industry by government increased to 55 percent.
2. 1975: Decree 6 increased federal government share in oil sector to 80 percent, with only 20 percent going to states.
3. 1976: First exploration and development venture by NNOC undertaken and drills to uncover commercial quantities of petroleum off-shore.
4. 1978: Perhaps most importantly, the federal government created the Land Use Act which vested control over state lands in control of military governors appointed by the federal military regime, and eventually led to Section 40(3) of the 1979 Constitution which declared all minerals, oil, natural gas, and natural resources found within the bounds of Nigeria to be legal property of the Nigerian federal government.

5. 1979: In an effort to establish further control over the industry, the government merges and restructures the NNOC and the Ministry of Petroleum to form the Nigeria National Petroleum Corporation (NNPC), an entity which would exert more power over the allocation and sale of concessions than the NNOC. By 1979, the NNPC had also gained 60 percent participation in the oil industry.

Conflict in the Niger Delta

Following the suppression of the short-lived Adaka Boro revolt in the 1960s, the conflict in the Niger Delta over the skewed nature of the oil industry arose in the early 1990s due to tensions between the foreign oil corporations, the Nigerian federal government, and a number of the Niger Delta's ethnic groups who felt they were being exploited, particularly minority groups like the Ogoni as well as the Ijaw in the late 1990s. Ethnic and political unrest continued throughout the 1990s and persisted as of 2006 despite the conversion to a more democratic, civilian federal system under the Obasanjo government in 1999; democracy has, to some degree, fanned the flames as politicians seeking office may now employ militia groups to coerce voters and generally disrupt the election process. Competition for oil wealth fuelled violence between innumerable ethnic groups, causing the militarisation of nearly the entire region by ethnic militia groups as well as Nigerian military and police forces (notably the Nigerian Mobile Police). Victims of crimes were fearful of seeking justice for crimes committed against them because of growing "impunity from prosecution for individuals responsible for serious human rights abuses, [which] has created a devastating cycle of increasing conflict and violence". The regional and ethnic conflicts were so numerous that fully detailing each is impossible and impractical.

Joint Venture Companies

Most petroleum production and exploration is done under the auspices of joint ventures between foreign multinational corporations and the Nigerian federal government. This joint venture is driven by the Nigeria National Petroleum Corporation, a nationalised state corporation. All companies operating in Nigeria are compelled to obey government operational rules and naming conventions (companies operating in Nigeria must legally be sub-entities of the main corporation, often incorporating "Nigeria" into its name). Joint ventures account for approximately 95 percent of all crude oil output, while local independent companies operating in marginal fields account for the remaining 5 percent. Additionally, the Nigerian constitution states that all minerals, oil and gas legally belong to the federal government. Six companies are operating in Nigeria and are listed with their countries of origin as follows:

Royal Dutch Shell (British/Dutch)

Shell Petroleum Development Company of Nigeria Limited (SPDC), usually known simply as Shell Nigeria: a joint venture operated by Shell accounts for 50 percent of Nigerian's total oil production (899,000 bbl/d (142,900 m3/d) in 1997) from more than 80 oil fields. The joint venture is composed of NNPC (55 percent), Shell (30 percent), Total (10 percent) and (NAOC) Agip (5 percent) and operates largely onshore on dry land or in the mangrove swamp in the Niger Delta. The company has more than 100 producing oil fields, and a network of more than 6,000 kilometres of pipelines, flowing through 87 flow stations. SPDC operates two coastal oil export terminals. The Shell joint venture produces about 50 percent of Nigeria's total crude. Shell Nigeria owns concessions on four companies, namely, Shell Petroleum Development Company (SPDC), Shell Nigeria Exploration and Production Company (SNEPCO), Shell Nigeria Gas (SNG), Shell Nigeria Oil Products (SNOP), as well as holding a major stake in Nigeria Liquefied Natural Gas (NLNG). Shell formerly operated alongside British Petroleum as Shell-BP, but BP has since sold all of its Nigerian concessions. Most of Shell's operations in Nigeria are conducted through the Shell Petroleum Development Company (SPDC).

Chevron (American)

Chevron Nigeria Limited (CNL): A joint venture between NNPC (60 percent) and Chevron (40 percent) has in the past been the second largest producer (approximately 400,000 bbl/d (64,000 m3/d)), with fields located in the Warri region west of the Niger River and offshore in shallow water. It is reported to aim to increase production to 600,000 bbl/d (95,000 m3/d).

Exxon-Mobil (American)

Mobil Producing Nigeria Unlimited (MPNU): A joint venture between the NNPC (60 percent) and Exxon-Mobil (40 percent) operates in shallow water off Akwa Ibom state in the south-eastern delta and averaged production of 632,000 bbl/d (100,500 m3/d) in 1997, making it the second largest producer, as against 543,000 bpd in 1996. Mobil also holds a 50 percent interest in a Production Sharing Contract for a deep water block further offshore, and is reported to plan to increase output to 900,000 bbl/d (140,000 m3/d) by 2000. Oil industry sources indicate that Mobil is likely to overtake Shell as the largest producer in Nigeria within the next five years, if current trends continue, mainly due to its offshore base allowing it refuge from the strife Shell has experienced onshore. It operates in Nigeria under the subsidiary of Mobil Producing Nigeria (MPN).

Agip (Italian)

Nigerian Agip Oil Company Limited (NAOC): a joint venture operated by Agip and owned by the NNPC (60 percent), Agip (20 percent) and ConocoPhillips (20 percent) produces 150,000 bbl/d (24,000 m3/d) mostly from small onshore fields.

Total (French)

Total Petroleum Nigeria Limited (TPNL): a joint venture between NNPC (60 percent) and Elf (now Total) produced approximately 125,000 bbl/d (19,900 m3/d) during 1997, both on and offshore. Elf and Mobil are in dispute over operational control of an offshore field with a production capacity of 90,000 bbl/d (14,000 m3/d).

Texaco (now merged with Chevron)

NNPC Texaco-Chevron Joint Venture (formerly Texaco Overseas Petroleum Company of Nigeria Unlimited): a joint venture operated by Texaco and owned by NNPC (60 percent), Texaco (20 percent) and Chevron (20 percent) currently produces about 60,000 bbl/d (9,500 m3/d) from five offshore fields.

Current Situation

On account largely of the disruptions occasioned by the skewed nature of the oil industry in Nigeria, a lot of the foreign oil majors have been finding it very difficult to operate in the critical upstream sector. This is particularly the situation in the Niger-Delta region. After years of supporting the military to enforce more law and order in the region, the strategy has now shifted to divesting from highly exposed production sites, leaving indigenous and newly established "local content" firms like Seplat Petroleum Development Company and Britannia-U to take a bigger piece of the oil prospecting pie.

However, while Nigeria's oil revenue has totalled $340 billion in exports since the 1970s and it is the fifth largest producer, 70 percent of her population live on less than $1 a day, and 43 percent have no access to clean water. Though Nigeria is a major oil exporter, she imports most of her gasoline, and when fuel subsidies were removed in January 2012, fuel prices increased from roughly $1.70 per gallon to $3.50. Nigeria seems to be well set up – she produces a form of oil ideal for the United States, has huge reserves, and has increased her production to 2.8 million barrels of oil a day. But this, some say, is all a resource curse that is hurting Nigeria and to the disadvantage of her people, in addition to increasing strides in the development of alternative energy sources that make the days of "oil as king of the sector" to be numbered.

Oil Theft

A report analysing the effect of oil theft in Nigeria revealed in July 2013 that Nigeria lost out on $10.9 billion in potential oil revenues between 2009 and 2011.

Environmental Impact

The Niger Delta comprises 70,000 km² of wetlands formed primarily by sediment deposition. Home to 20 million people and 40 different ethnic groups, this floodplain makes up 7.5 percent of Nigeria's total landmass. It is the largest wetland and maintains the third-largest drainage area in Africa. The Delta's environment can be broken down into four ecological zones: coastal barrier islands, mangrove swamp forests, freshwater swamps, and lowland rainforests. This incredibly well-endowed ecosystem contains one of the highest concentrations of biodiversity on the planet, in addition to supporting the abundant flora and fauna, arable terrain that can sustain a wide variety of crops, economic trees, and more species of freshwater fish than any ecosystem in West Africa. The region could experience a loss of 40 percent of its inhabitable terrain in the next 30 years because of extensive dam construction in the region. The carelessness of the oil industry has also precipitated this situation, which can perhaps be best encapsulated by a 1983 report issued by the NNPC, long before popular unrest surfaced:

> The country witnessed the slow poisoning of its waters and the destruction of vegetation and agricultural land by oil spills which occur during petroleum operations. But since the inception of the oil industry in Nigeria, more than twenty-five years ago, there has been no concerned and effective effort on the part of the government, let alone the oil operators, to control environmental problems associated with the industry.

Oil Spill and Water Contamination

Oil spill in Nigeria is a common occurrence. It has been estimated that between nine million to 13 million barrels have been spilled since oil drilling started in 1958. The government estimates that about 7,000 spills occurred between 1970 and 2000. Causes include corrosion of pipelines and tankers (accounts for 50 percent of all spills), sabotage (28 percent), and oil production operations (21 percent), with 1 percent of the spills being accounted for by inadequate or non-functional production equipment. A reason that corrosion accounts for such a high percentage of all spills is that as a result of the small size of the oilfields in the Niger Delta, there is an extensive network of pipelines between the fields. Many facilities and pipelines have been constructed to older standards, poorly maintained and outlived their estimated life span. Sabotage is performed primarily through what is known as "bunkering", whereby the saboteur taps a pipeline and in the process of extraction sometimes the pipeline is damaged. Oil extracted in this manner can often be sold for cash compensation.

Oil spillage has a major impact on the ecosystem. Large tracts of the mangrove forests, which are especially susceptible to oil (this is mainly because it is stored in the soil and re-released annually with inundation), have been destroyed. An estimated 5-10 percent of Nigerian mangrove ecosystems have been wiped out either by settlement or oil. Spills take out crops and aquacultures through contamination of the groundwater and soils. Drinking water is also frequently contaminated and a sheen of oil is visible in many localised bodies of water. If the drinking water is contaminated, even if no immediate health effects are apparent, the numerous hydrocarbons and chemicals present in oil represent a carcinogenic risk. Offshore spills, which are usually much greater in scale, contaminate coastal environments and cause a decline in local fishing production. Nigerian regulations are weak and rarely enforced allowing oil companies, in essence, to self-regulate.

Natural Gas Flaring

Nigeria flares more natural gas associated with oil extraction than any other country, with estimates suggesting that of the 3.5 billion cubic feet (99,000,000 m3) of associated gas (AG) produced annually, 2.5 billion cubic feet (71,000,000 m3), or about 70 percent is wasted via flaring. Statistical data associated with gas flaring is notoriously unreliable. But AG wasted during flaring is estimated to cost Nigeria US $2.5 billion on a yearly basis. Companies operating in Nigeria harvest natural gas for commercial purposes, however, prefer to extract its gas from deposits where it is found in isolation as non-associated gas. It is costly to separate commercially viable associated gas from oil, hence gas flaring to increase crude production.

Gas flaring is discouraged by the international community as it contributes to climate change. In fact, in Western Europe 99 percent of associated gas is used or re-injected into the ground. Gas flaring in Nigeria releases large amounts of methane, which has very high global warming potential. The methane is accompanied by carbon dioxide, of which Nigeria is estimated to have emitted more than

34.38 million tons in 2002, accounting for about 50 percent of all industrial emissions in the country and 30 percent of the total CO_2 emissions. As flaring in the west has been minimised, in Nigeria it has grown proportionally with oil production. While the international community, the Nigerian government and the oil corporations seem to agree that gas flaring need to be curtailed, efforts to do so have been slow and largely ineffective.

Gas flares release a variety of potentially poisonous chemicals such as nitrogen dioxides, sulphur dioxide, volatile organic compounds like benzene, toluene, xylene and hydrogen sulfide, as well as carcinogens like benzapyrene and dioxins. Often, gas flares are often close to local communities and lack adequate fencing or protection for villagers who may risk nearing the heat of the flare in order to carry out their daily activities. Flares which are often older and inefficient are rarely relocated away from villages, and are known to coat the land and communities in the area with soot and damage adjacent vegetation.

In November 2005, a judgment by the Federal High Court of Nigeria ordered that gas flaring must stop in a Niger Delta community as it violates guaranteed constitutional rights to life and dignity. In a case brought against the Shell Petroleum Development Company of Nigeria (Shell), Justice C. V. Nwokorie ruled in Benin City that the damaging and wasteful practice of flaring cannot lawfully continue.

In the *Civilising Mission* of April 30, 2010, there is a piece on the subject of "A Nigerian Oil Curse" written by J.F. Gjersø. In it, he says:

> There are often references being made to the oil curse, the supposed wretchedness of resource endowments that plunges developing countries into a never-ending spiral of internal strife and instability. The rationale is partially based upon the developing countries' weak institutional framework which makes states harbouring valuable extractible resources susceptible to predation from external or internal factions. But there is also an economic aspect, the

export commodities inflates the domestic exchange rate to the detriment of manufacturing sectors, making these less competitive. Over-reliance on a poorly diversified portfolio of export commodities also makes the economy highly susceptible to market volatility, as commodities such as crude oil, minerals or agricultural produce etc are subject to frequently changing international price fluctuations.

An example of such reliance would be Africa's largest crude oil producer Nigeria. At 2.17 million bbls/day (2008, BP Statistical Review, 2009), Nigeria is a substantial supplier of oil known as Bonny Light, a gasoline-rich crude, favoured among primarily American refineries for its high quality (49.7 percent of Nigerian exports, 2008), making it inexpensive to refine. With daily exports running at approximately 2 million bbls/day, two very large crude carriers (VLCCs) are required for tran-shipment. Nigeria has also seen falling apparent consumption levels over the last ten years, currently standing at around 200,000 bbls/day.

Nigerian Crude Oil Production, Exports and Apparent Consumption

At the time of the above report, Nigerian oil production was, however, not running at total capacity due to guerrilla activities shutting in approximately 0.5 million bbls/day. This was the result of the long-standing insurgency conducted by the Movement for the Emancipation of the Niger Delta (MEND) and other militant groups destroying pipelines and attacking installation infrastructure and crew. They had stated that they were fighting for a more equitable sharing of the oil revenues, with a greater portion being earmarked directly to the producing region. Additionally, a stated goal was to lower pollution levels from the production facilities and reducing Nigeria's dependence on foreign companies to extract the oil wealth. However, some commentators likened their activities to opportunist banditry. The response from the oil companies operating in the Niger Delta has been to employ floating production, storage and offloading (FPSOs) units to gain mobility should the conflict escalate into a large-scale war, to lobby the Nigerian government for added military protection and to hire private security firms. Despite the Nigerian government's counter-insurgency tactics, the guerrillas were quite successful in conducting their activities since the early 1990s, something that might illustrate their resilience. And in response, an amnesty programme was to be brokered where repentant militants were encouraged to sign up for a rehabilitation and reintegration scheme, complete with monthly allowances and re-training.

Even though Nigeria suffers some negative consequences of her resource endowment, the positive aspects in the form of export earnings more than makes up for it, as is clearly visible from the GDP per capita graph. In periods of high international oil prices, revenue from oil exports should be diverted to building more sustainable manufacturing sectors and into increasing the overall education level of the population. More resources should also be diverted to the producing regions in an attempt to reduce the recruitment incentive for the guerrilla movements. Should the Nigerian government succeed in pacifying the insurgents, an additional 0.5 million bbls/day in production capacity would be freed, increasing total production by 20 percent, in 2008, that would have meant $20 billion on an annual basis.

On its part, the *Wikipedia* profile on the petroleum industry in Nigeria as extracted in February 2014 reads:

> The petroleum industry in Nigeria, Africa is the largest industry and main generator of GDP in the continent's most populous nation. Since the discovery of oil in the Niger Delta in the late 1950s, the oil industry has been marred by political and economic strife due to a long history of corrupt military regimes and the complicity of multinational corporations, notably Royal Dutch Shell. However it was not until the early 1990s, after the Nigerian state execution of playwright and activist Ken Saro-Wiwa, that the situation was given international attention, leading to the immediate suspension of Nigeria from the

Commonwealth of Nations. Nigeria is identified as a major concern regarding human rights and environmental degradation by the international community and the firms that operate there. The Nigerian government, oil corporations, and oil-dependent Western countries have been criticised as too slow to implement reforms aimed at aiding a desperately underdeveloped area and remediating the unsustainable environmental degradation that petroleum extraction has caused.

=In February 2013, the Nigerian Association of Chambers of Commerce, Industry, Mines and Agriculture (NACCIMA) claimed that the oil sector of the country "is killing the economy". NACCIMA's Director General at the time, Dr. John Isemede said the oil sector is affecting businesses in the country negatively by failing to add real value to them. He said the oil sector has caused substantial decline in agricultural exports, which began in the mid-1960s and continued to date.

Oil Discovery

Developers in the pursuit of commercially available oil struck it big in 1956. Prior to the discovery of oil, Nigeria, like many other African countries, strongly relied on agricultural exports to other countries to supply their economy. In fact, that was what many Nigerians thought the developers were looking for - palm oil. But after nearly 50 years searching for oil in the country, Shell-BP discovered oil at Oloibiri in the Niger Delta. Wishing to utilise this newfound oil opportunity, the first oil field began production in 1958. After that, the economy of Nigeria would have seemingly experienced a strong increase. However, competition for the profits that oil produces has created a great level of terror and conflict for those living in the region. Citizens of Nigeria believe that they haven't been able to see the economic benefits of oil companies. Additionally, because the Nigerian government has remained the majority shareholder in the profits created by the production of Nigerian oil, this leads to citizens insisting that oil companies should directly compensate the people.

Production and Exploration

As of 2000, oil and gas exports accounted for more than 98% of export earnings and about 83% of federal government revenue, as well as generating more than 14% of its GDP. It also provides 95% of foreign exchange earnings, and about 65% of government budgetary revenues.

Nigeria's proven oil reserves are estimated by the United States Energy Information Administration (EIA) at between 16 and 22 billion barrels, but other sources claim there could be as much as 35.3 billion barrels (5.61×109 m3). Its reserves make Nigeria the tenth most petroleum-rich nation, and by the far the most affluent in Africa. In mid-2001 its crude oil production was averaging around 2.2 million barrels (350,000 m^3) per day

Nearly all of the country's primary reserves are concentrated in and around the delta of the Niger River, but off-shore rigs are also prominent in the well-endowed coastal region. Nigeria is one of the few major oil-producing nations still capable of increasing its oil output. Unlike most of the other OPEC countries, Nigeria is not projected to exceed peak production until at least 2009[citation needed]. The reason for Nigeria's relative unproductivity is primarily OPEC regulations on production to regulate prices on the international market. More recently, production has been disrupted intermittently by the protests of the Niger Delta's inhabitants, who feel they are being exploited.

Nigeria has a total of 159 oil fields and 1481 wells in operation according to the Ministry of Petroleum Resources. The most productive region of the nation is the coastal Niger Delta Basin in the Niger Delta or "South-south" region which encompasses 78 of the 159 oil fields. Most of Nigeria's oil fields are small and scattered, and as of 1990, these small unproductive fields accounted for 62.1% of all Nigerian production. This contrasts with the sixteen largest fields which produced 37.9% of Nigeria's petroleum at that time. As a result of the numerous small fields, an extensive and well-developed pipeline network has been engineered to transport the crude. Also due to the lack of highly productive fields, money from the jointly operated (with the federal government) companies is constantly directed towards petroleum exploration and production.

Nigeria's petroleum is classified mostly as "light" and "sweet", as the oil is largely free of sulphur. Nigeria is the largest producer of sweet oil in OPEC. This sweet oil is similar in composition to petroleum extracted from the North Sea. This crude oil is known as "Bonny light". Names of other Nigerian crudes, all of which are named according to export terminal, are Qua Ibo, Escravos blend, Brass River, Forcados, and Pennington Anfan.

The US remains the largest importer of Nigeria's crude oil, accounting for 40% of the country's total oil exports. Nigeria provides about 10% of overall U.S. oil imports and ranks as the fifth-largest source for oil imports in the U.S.

There are six petroleum exportation terminals in the country. Shell owns two, while Mobil, Chevron, Texaco, and Agip own one each. Shell also owns the Forcados Terminal, which is capable of storing 13 million barrels (2,100,000 m3) of crude oil in conjunction with the nearby Bonny Terminal. Mobil operates primarily out of the Qua Iboe Terminal in Akwa Ibom State, while Chevron owns the Escravos Terminal located in Delta State and has a storage capacity of 3.6 million barrels (570,000 m3). Agip operates the Brass Terminal in Brass, a town 113 km southwest of Port Harcourt and has a storage capacity of 3,558,000 barrels (565,700 m3). Texaco operates the Pennington Terminal.

Offshore

Oil companies in Africa investigate offshore production as an alternative area of production. Deepwater production mainly involves underwater drilling that exists 400 m or more below the surface of the water. By expanding to deep water drilling the possible sources for finding new oil reserves is expanded. Through the introduction of deep water drilling 50% more oil is extracted than before the new forms of retrieving the oil. Angola and Nigeria are the largest oil producers in Africa. In Nigeria, the deepwater sector still has a large avenue to expand and develop. The amount of oil extracted from Nigeria is expected to expand from 15,000 bbl/d (2,400 m3/d) in 2003 to 1.27 mbbl/d (202,000 m3/d) in 2010. Deepwater drilling for oil is especially attractive to oil companies because the Nigerian government has very little share in these activities and it is more difficult for the government to regulate the offshore activities of the companies. Also, the deepwater extraction plants are less disturbed by local militant attacks, seizures due to civil conflicts, and sabotage. These advancements offer more resources and alternatives to extract the oil from the Niger Delta, with hopefully less conflict than the operations on land.

Natural Gas

Natural gas reserves are well over 187 trillion ft^3 (2,800 km^3), the gas reserves are three times as substantial as the crude oil reserves. The biggest natural gas initiative is the Nigerian Liquefied Natural Gas Company, which is operated jointly by several companies and the state. It began exploration and production in 1999. Chevron is also attempting to create the Escravos Gas Utilization project which will be capable of producing 160 million standard ft^3 of gas per day.

There is also a gas pipeline, known as the West African Gas Pipeline, in the works but has encountered numerous setbacks. The pipeline would allow for transportation of natural gas to Benin, Ghana, Togo, and Cote d'Ivoire. The majority of Nigeria's natural gas is flared off and it is estimated that Nigeria loses 18.2 million US$ daily from the loss of the flared gas.

Downstream

Nigeria's total petroleum refining capacity is 445,000 barrels per day (70,700 m3/d); however, only 240,000 bbl/d (38,000 m3/d) was allotted during the 1990s. Subsequently crude oil production for refineries was reduced further to as little as 75,000 bbl/d (11,900 m3/d) during the regime of Sani Abacha. There are four major oil refineries: the Warri Refinery and Petrochemical Plant which can refine 125,000 barrels (19,900 m3) of crude per day, the New Port Harcourt Refinery which can produce 150,000 barrels per day (24,000 m3/d) (there is also an 'Old' Port Harcourt

Refinery with negligible production), as well as the now defunct Kaduna Refinery. The Port Harcourt and Warri Refineries both operate at only 30% capacity.

It is estimated that demand and consumption of petroleum in Nigeria grows at a rate of 12.8% annually. However, petroleum products are unavailable to most Nigerians and are quite costly, because almost all of the oil extracted by the multinational oil companies is refined overseas, while only a limited quantity is supplied to Nigerians themselves.

Current Production

Nigeria is Africa's largest oil producer and has been a member of the Organization of Petroleum Exporting Countries since 1971. The Nigerian economy is heavily dependent on the oil sector, which, accounts for over 95 percent of export earnings and about 40 percent of government revenues, according to the International Monetary Fund. According to the International Energy Agency, Nigeria produced about 2.53 million barrels per day, well below its oil production capacity of over 3 million barrels per day, in 2011. Nigeria is an important oil supplier to the United States. For the last nine years, the United States has imported between 9-11 percent of its crude oil from Nigeria; however, United States import data for the first half of 2012 show that Nigerian crude is down to a 5 percent share of total United States crude imports. According to the International Energy Agency, in 2011, approximately 33 percent of Nigeria's crude exports were sent to the United States, making Nigeria its fourth largest foreign oil supplier. Although total crude imports into the United States are falling, imports from Nigeria have declined at a steeper rate, according to the International Energy Agency. The main reasons underlying this trend are that some Gulf Coast refiners have reduced Nigerian imports in favour of domestically-produced crude, and that two refineries in the U.S. East Coast, which were significant buyers of Nigerian crude, were idled in late 2011. As a result, Nigerian crude as a share of total United States imports has fallen to 5 percent in the first half of 2012, down from 10 and 11 percent in the first half of 2011 and 2010, respectively, according to the International Energy Agency. According to the CIA World Factbook, Nigeria's main export partners are the United States, India, Brazil, Spain, France and the Netherlands. Shell has been working in Nigeria since 1936, and currently dominates gas production in the country, as the Niger Delta, which contains most of Nigeria's gas resources, also houses most of Shell's hydrocarbon assets.

Where the Wealth should now go

Fortunately for Nigeria, our oil story is not over yet. However, the discovery of shale, investments in other massive oil alternatives by many countries that depended almost solely on oil is a veritable wake-up call to oily laggards as this self-acclaimed "giant of Africa". It is time to frontally begin to wipe away the *shibboleths* and let only the truth stand.

First, oil has become some opium. It is said that the last person to recognise bad breath is the sufferer himself. Economic managers in Nigeria and their allies, the political leaders, need to step back to see how almost hopelessly dependent Nigeria is on oil. It is a crisis. Nothing brings this to the fore than during the yearly budget ritual where the National assembly and the Ministry of Finance are brick-batting over what price to adopt as benchmark price. It is indeed the height of how low we have sunk as a nation that our entire economic process continues to be driven by external factors over which we barely have any control. And so it is between ensuring a semblance of budgetary balance and getting more of the resources spent on a few more national development projects.

In our humble view, both sides are wrong. The way to proceed is to develop a big vision development picture and work with a framework that would corral all revenues into serving this vision. In doing this, we would have to be holistic and comprehensive. What does the country, its economy and citizens need this year? What about next? What about in five, ten, twenty, fifty and hundred years time? This kind of focus would take away a lot of the pressure on the economic managers today to earn and spend. And in such a climate, we find that not much is usually achieved.

After this has been done, we can then break it down to the specific areas of need that would in turn boost value creation for the nation. Make no mistake about it; for wealth to make sense, it must be re-invested in further wealth creation schemes. And for a nation, the greatest wealth streams are her people who would then go on to create even more wealth for the nation.

We must thus invest in ensuring that the people are in a position to produce even the wealth we need. To do this we must ensure that today's tranche of wealth which is largely derived from oil is invested in producing healthy and active citizens who benefit from:

1. a strong emphasis on maternal and child health. A few states today, Delta State included, provide free and maternal healthcare to pregnant women, nursing mothers and children aged 0-5. This is good and needs to be built upon;
2. universal citizens health coverage through a viable health insurance scheme, etc, complete with functional and affordable health services provided by well trained professionals working in well-equipped hospitals;
3. good shelter for all;
4. a life-sustaining educational system that provides the young and indeed all citizens with skills needed to enter the job market as employees or entrepreneurs with corresponding provisions for further and life-long learning and career adaptability;
5. critical investments in economic areas where the nation has competitive advantage. The first one is not difficult; it is

the petrochemical sector, from planning to management, to upstream, to downstream and then ancillary and post-process and para-industrial areas. This has become even most critical now that some of Nigeria's major patrons in the crude oil export trade have made very solid and significant strides in the development of either their own oil and gas fields or in the development of alternative technologies such as Shale oil in the Northern American hemisphere;

6. following the money and income substitution. In our inter-dependent world today, it is important that scarce foreign exchange be only deployed to critical need areas that the country absolutely cannot produce locally. We need to track where our foreign exchange resources are presently deployed and begin to take steps to ensure that this goal is rigorously followed upon and with great discipline at that.

Nigeria today imports a lot of things that with the right government policies would be produced here in the country. Let us start with agricultural and food produce. Then, we move on to even industrial goods such as clothing, cars, building materials and the likes. The truth is that a lot of things that are presently imported now will be produced using the right mix of carrot and stick measures. What is required is the political will to chart out the path and to follow through. This is what we missed and this is what we need to get back.

Reform and Restructuring of the NNPC

We cannot bring this discussion of Nigeria's oily misfortunes to a close without closely reviewing the operations and presence of the country's central oil sector player through the years, the Nigerian National Petroleum Corporation (NNPC). Established in 1971, first as the Nigeria National Oil Company (NNOC), the NNPC is the single most important player in the nation's oil fortunes.

With arms like the Department of Petroleum Resources (DPR), the Corporation oversees both the upstream and downstream operations of the country. Through the DPR, it allocates acreages to potential crude oil exploration firms and also manages the refineries as well as the importation of refined petroleum products as well as the export of crude oil.

It also is engaged in ancillary activities in the sector through or alongside other agencies like the Petroleum Technology Development Fund, the PPPRA and NAPIMS. The NNPC is indeed a virtual behemoth whose grip over the petroleum industry in Nigeria is near-choking.

Understandably, the Corporation has been in the firing line as the principal villain in Nigeria's oily troubles. And successive administrations at the Corporation have not escaped the umbrage of the public given widespread perception that it operates essentially as a slush fund which successive administrations have used and continue to use to feather their own nests and those of their friends.

While the negative perception of the NNPC has almost been there since its inception, it is also true that progressively the poor perception and scale of the problem has worsened over time. During the Obasanjo military administration, the talk was of ₦2.8b missing. In the Babangida era, it was of unexplained "Gulf war" funds. Now, we have issues and allegations of unremitted funds for products duly sold by an NNPC subsidiary, unapproved kerosene subsidy payments and a fuel subsidy scam.

Indeed, in the contemporary history of Nigeria, there may not be any firm that has been as heavily pilloried as the NNPC. The NNPC would, therefore, have to be thoroughly re-invented.

Here also we would need to look outside Nigerian shores to see the examples from several other climes where state-oil firms have continued to play a very deserving role in the promotion of their oil industry and indeed in the overall economic development of the nation. For example, we have the example of Norway already referred to. But we also have Petrobas in Brazil which has so commendably engaged in extensive research and development, culminating in the widespread blending of ethanol and related biofuels into the petroleum refining process. There is equally the example of

Venezuela which, in the Chavez era, not only deployed very strong political will in renegotiating all of the extant contract agreements in the sector that had hitherto favoured foreign multinational players, it equally embarked on a widespread scheme of establishing off-shore refineries in markets outside her national borders as part of a determined drive to secure a greater chunk of the profits from the upstream sector.

Fundamental to our contemplated reforms, therefore, would be a total policy and philosophy orientation. From the era of the military rulers, one of the primary policy failures in the sector has been to focus on how much earnings the country could garner from the resource. Till date, not much has changed. At the National Assembly every year, several weeks are spent agreeing on a draft benchmark price and total production quotas. While there is nothing fundamentally wrong with extensively debating what and how to deal with revenues emanating from the sector, we would rather counsel a renewed focus on ensuring a more sustainable and integrated exploitation of the resource with a view to getting more and more from a product with high net-worth value.

To underscore the import of this shift, we would need to introduce entirely new paradigms that would encompass personnel, structural and organisational changes. One such urgent challenge would involve the prompt and decisive passage of a most beneficial Petroleum Industry Bill that would form the nucleus for other reforms that would be introduced and which would help jumpstart some of the more radical changes that would address some of the other system paradoxes. For example, rather than have a well-developed and competently staffed petroleum desk in the Ministry of Industry supervising oil operations in the country, we have created a very powerful grade A ministry that largely presides over sleaze and graft.

The proper way to go now, in our view, is to break down the details and approach the industry for what it is: economic and industrial activity. A lot of the politics has to be cut off and just like is currently being done with energy sector reform, the petroleum industry has to be managed as business and industrial operations with emphasis on return on investment, efficiency and continuous process improvement. The telecoms reforms of about a decade now have led the country from a 20, 000 telephone line coverage to over one hundred million lines. It has cut off a lot of the graft, brought in a fresh 10 percent in GDP growth and though there remain service delivery and network efficiency issues, the market would invariably address that. This is equally the way to go for the petroleum sector.

In doing this, one point that will be raised as a reason why not to go this way is the issue of national security, national pride and the fact that petroleum straddles almost all tiers of the nation. But these issues are themselves not an obstacle or a deterrent to the reform being contemplated.

Security was an issue for not deregulating the radio and telecommunications sector in the country. But we have since found out that the answer did not lie in continuing to stifle the media terrain but in a strengthened regulator, in the form of the National Broadcasting Commission. We can similarly strengthen agencies like the Department of Petroleum Resources, NAPIMS and the NNPC to ensure that they are strong regulators instead of the current situation of a plethora of under-performing state-run organisations who promote less-than-adequate results annually and whose perennial problems cannot truly be fixed today even as we continue to hide under the dubious cover of "national" interest. Pray, since when did national interest become synonymous with mediocrity? This is the critical challenge for Nigeria today.

9

Saving the Future:
The Challenge of a New Nigeria

Introduction

Recently, Nigeria marked a hundred years of the amalgamation, by the British Empire, of the Lagos Colony, its Northern and Southern Protectorates into one country in January 1914. Since the amalgamation, historians and public affairs analysts have tried to explain why this amalgamation was necessary in the first place. Reasons put forward have ranged from economic to political considerations, with some more creative commentators giving a devious slant to the discussion. However, what can be gleaned from Lord Frederick Lugar's proclamation speech, as well as his dispatches to Her Majesty's Government of the day in the United Kingdom, was that the amalgamation was as much an economic decision as well as political and administrative one that suited or tied in with the "Agenda" of the British Empire. A hundred years on, the issue of national agenda is still fraught with challenges and unfulfilled dreams.

Post-Amalgamation Years

The years following the amalgamation saw the colonial government consolidate the sovereignty of the British Government over Nigeria. The country was divided into three regions: Eastern, Western and Northern Regions and governed through an indirect system of government that recognised limited authority for indigenous traditional rulers. Key to the success of this system of indirect administration and perhaps an early recognition of the deep differences amongst the indigenes of the unified country was the modified system of indirect rule which was successful because in practice, British administrative procedures under indirect rule entailed constant interaction between colonial authorities and local rulers - the system was modified to fit the needs of each region. In the north, for instance, legislation took the form of a decree cosigned by the governor and the emir, while in the south, the governor sought the approval of the Legislative Council.[5]

Central to the differences amongst the regions were religion, ethnicity, culture, early access to western education and a proclivity for enterprise. In the years that followed the amalgamation and leading to nationalism and independence, these differences became deeper and wider. They defined pre- independence partisan politics, constitutional conferences, national census exercises, elections and virtually every facet of national life. Ultimately, it would lead to two military coups and a 30-month civil war shortly after independence. But by then, the colonial government had been dismantled, its agenda no longer feasible in an independent Nigeria. The question is: "In the ensuing void, what was the alternative agenda of these disparate groups of nationalities?"

The National Agenda

Nigeria wants to be a great country. Her political and business leaders have said as much and many Nigerians share this aspiration. After missing the year 2000 target set by almost all administrations before then, to provide everything from food, shelter and jobs, to a happy life for all, etc, the country briefly focused on being the poster country for achieving all of UN Millennium Development Goals (MDGs) by 2015. After that came Vision 20:2020, an initiative with unclear methodology that seeks to position Nigeria as a top 20 economy by the year 2020, which is six years away. Beyond that, we also appear anxious to overtake South Africa as the largest economy in sub-Saharan Africa. Hopefully, with the rebasing of our GDP in 2014, we should achieve this or be close to doing this. Thereafter, we can be happy that we have a bigger economy than South Africa,

---

5   *Nigeria: A Country Study*, Washington: GPO for the Library of Congress, 1991.

even if the South African economy is eminently more productive and diversified with a base that looks more sustainable than ours.

Our obsession with being great and the paradox it presents is better captured by the late Professor Chinua Achebe who noted that "one of the commonest manifestations of underdevelopment is a tendency among the ruling elite to live in a world of make believe and unrealistic expectations".[6] He illustrated this with the contrasting comments, in 1979, of the ex-Chancellor of West Germany and the soon-to-be ex-Military head of state of Nigeria, respectively, as follows:

> Germany is not a world power, it does not wish to be a world power.
>
> *Helmut Schmidt, June 1979.*
>
> Nigeria will become one of the ten leading nations in the world by the turn of the century.
>
> *Olusegun Obasanjo, August 1979.*

Needless to say, this is 13 years after the turn of the century and Nigeria is not yet one of the ten leading nations in the world. She has, instead changed her mantra to focus on being one of the 20 leading economies by year 2020, a goal which she seems not to be actively pursuing and which may have fallen through the cracks. A unified Germany, on the other hand, has turned out to be the economic bedrock of the European Union and one of the countries least affected by the global crises of 2008-2010 because of careful economic planning, productivity and discipline of the Germans.

Back to the issue of agenda: if we are all agreed that we desire Nigeria to be a great country, what should be on our collective agenda for the country?

---

6   Chinua Achebe(2000), *The Trouble with Nigeria*, Fourth Dimension Publishing Co.

Nationalism and Governance

Nationalism in Nigeria has proved to be a difficult prospect as most times, the ethnic nationalities that make up the country are engaged in a bitter and, sometimes, bloody contest for power, resources or supremacy of ideology. As noted by Max Siollun,

> Nigeria was so ethnically, religiously and linguistically complex that even some of its leading politicians initially doubted it could constitute a real country. The cultural differences between the ethnic groups made it virtually impossible for Nigerians to have any commonality of purpose. Party politics (and political parties) took on the identity and ideology of each of the three geo-political regions in the north, south-east and south-west.[7]

It is true that when there is the odd international sporting competition, there seems to be burning nationalism in most Nigerians. But this quickly dissipates when the contest is over and there is a reversion to the status quo.

The quest to give birth to "a Nigerian nationalism" amongst the citizens as well as to root out the blossoming seed of corruption was what prompted the first military coup in 1966. Introducing the coup, the coupists noted that

> The aim of the Revolutionary Council is to establish a strong united and prosperous nation, free from corruption and internal strife…. My dear countrymen, you will hear, and probably see a lot being done by certain bodies charged by the Supreme Council with the duties of national integration…Our enemies are ……. those that seek to keep the country divided permanently so that they can remain in office as ministers or VIPs at least, the tribalists, the nepotists,

---

[7]   Max Siollun (2009). Oil Politics and Violence: Nigeria's Military Coup culture (1966-1976), Algora Publishing.

those that make the country look big for nothing
before international circles.[8]

This coup itself was acknowledged to have failed for the very
reasons that it was staged - tribalism. Some of the soldiers sabotaged
the coup by refusing to eliminate, as agreed, some of the leaders
of their own ethnic groups. The whole events of January 1966 not
only drove deeper ill-will amongst the different ethnic groups in the
country, it was also the catalyst for a series of military coups and
military regimes for 29 out of the next 33 years. Additionally, it was
the trigger for the 30 months of civil war that claimed millions of
lives.

Between 1966 and 1999, there were at least nine coup d'états,
some successful, and the nation was largely under the grip of the
military. Usually, when a military coup is successful, the first casualty
is the Constitution. This slaying of the Constitution is then followed
by the promulgation of special decrees that give absolute power to
the coupists. Generally, as noted by Max Siollun, though the coup
speech is filled with lots of populist pronouncements at the time,
what really drives the execution of a coup is more of power grab
and resentment by a crop of military officers at perceived slights by
the ruling clique. True national interest is hardly ever in the mix.
We note that because most of the coupists grab power even when
unprepared, their attempt at governance is usually disastrous for the
following reasons:

1.   The cabinet is normally made up of members of "the inner
     circle" with some odd national or international figures
     thrown in to give it a sense of diversity and credibility. With
     this type of set up and an absence of checks and balances
     from a legislature or judiciary, there is a free reign of the
     whims of the soldiers.
2.   Because they come to office unprepared (this is still applicable
     in some cases in our current democracy), there is a long
     lead time in understanding the art of governance and what

---

8   Chukwuma K. Nzeogwu, Military Coup Speech, 1966.

constitutes national priorities, and usually, a counter coup topples the government before it even does this. Where it manages to stay for a reasonable length of time, it is preoccupied with quashing potential coups, phantom and real.

3. Because most military regimes have no real intention to return the country to democratic governance, they seek to perpetuate themselves in office. This is done by spending heavily on defence and other infrastructure for intimidating the populace, and voting substantial funds to propagate their cronies and supporters.

4. In response to a demand for performance, such regimes usually embark on populist and bogus infrastructural projects and economic programmes that are ill-advised, and end up as white elephant projects as soon as they leave office. The nation's physical and economic landscape is dotted with relics of some of the misadventures. The opportunity cost of this behaviour is that critical national services and infrastructure are denied funding. The lack of this causes stagnation in the socio economic wellbeing of citizens.

It would be wrong, however, to suggest that the military were solely responsible for the challenges to nationhood nor apportion most of the blame to them. The first military putsch was in response to a failure to weave a nation from the country by the civilian regime. Also, politicians have always collaborated with the military in governance and in fact did run the country between 1979 and 1983 when the country's economy almost collapsed amidst price crises in the international oil market.

Since 1999, there have been civilian governments in place, but the usual challenges of nepotism and governance have continued. These days, the deep ethnic and religious divisions are backed by armed and dangerous ethnic and religious militias that routinely issue threats and back these up with acts of violence and terror. The critical question that confronts us today is: "Can these issues be decisively tackled as we move into the second century as a country?"

Development and Social Welfare

At amalgamation and later, independence, Nigeria held out so much economic promise especially with the level of economic activity and productivity within her borders. The discovery of oil in the Niger Delta heightened expectations but disappoint-ments were to follow closely, with years of misapplication of funds accruing from oil revenue, virtual abandonment of other economic activities within the country and a descent into economic chaos.

In the past few years, however, despite absence of many public services and infrastructure, there has been cheery news about the country's gross domestic product (GDP) which has witnessed commendable growth, quarter on quarter, with 2013 Quarter 3 growth rate of 6.81 percent, according to the figures released by the National Bureau of Statistics. This growth in GDP, however, does not tell the story of our national development as it has not really translated to better life for citizens. The question then is: "What is national development?" To answer this, let us borrow a definition, which clarifies that

> national development refers to the ability of a country or countries to improve the social welfare of the people, for example, by providing social amenities like good education, infrastructure, medical care and social services.

For most economic planners, the burning question is what to target first: social welfare of the people or economic growth. It is certain everybody will not agree on a single answer. But it is instructive to note that many countries in Asia, South America and the Middle East that have attained relatively high standard of living over the past 40 years tended to target improvements in the quality of social welfare indicators. It is only after this that sustained economic growth was witnessed.

For us, looking at the national state of affairs of the indicators highlighted in the definition above, perhaps, illustrates where we need to pay a lot of attention in our national investments. Let us consider some of them below.

Education

On July 1, 2013, the Academic Staff Union of Universities (ASSU), the umbrella union for lecturers in Nigerian universities, commenced on an indefinite strike. A clear five months after, the strike was still on. At the root of their grouse with the federal government was the non-implementation of an agreement signed in 2009, in particular, and underfunding of Nigerian universities, in general. Predictably, when the strike was called off, students were rushed to examinations to make up for lost time.

The frequent ASUU strikes aside, if you pay attention to the news media and observe the quality of subject matter knowledge with many of the recent products of the tertiary institutions, you will be concerned about the system that has produced these graduates. But that is not where the problem begins. It starts at the primary school level which constitu-tionally is under the joint management of the states and local government councils. With the exception of a few states, if you are familiar with the mode of operation of the local government councils in the country, you will appreciate that they are not equipped for this very important task. When you add to that the quality and motivation of teachers at that level of education, you will understand the quality of the products from the public primary school system shepherded into secondary schools. Only recently in Edo State, a long standing primary school teacher could not read the material presented to her in an impromptu assessment by the Governor. The public secondary schools only reflect, on a larger scale, what happens at the primary level.

All these have led to a boom in highly priced private institutions which sometimes deliver services of dubious quality, catering to primary, secondary or tertiary education. The case by ASUU, therefore, while it may be valid in some ways, ignores the full educational value chain in the country. On the back of a promised ₦200 billion per year for the next five years, the strike was initially planned to be called off but was later continued as ASUU made additional demands after securing commitments for the funding mentioned earlier. The next question is: What happens to primary and secondary education? Is it all about funding? What worries me particularly about the proliferation of private universities is that the challenges go beyond funding to include availability and quality of faculty they can attract.

Medical Care

Perhaps, nothing defines our present health care system as the news article in *International Medical Travel Journal* which noted that in 2012 alone, 18,000 Nigerians spent ₦42 billion on medical tourism to India.[9] The article identified

> low standards of patient care, an absence of world-class hospitals and diagnostic centres and the stunted growth of the healthcare system in the country, as responsible for this massive medical tourism to India; A poor pipeline for high skills, poor health value chain, as well as low health insurance cover, have led to weak effective demand for healthcare services, resulting in poor economies of scale for hospital services in the country. Medical equipment in some hospitals is bedeviled with irregular maintenance and upgrades, and diagnostic services are not readily within reach, raising questions of quality control, availability, timeliness and reliability. Ambulatory services are often not available or affordable. There is an absence of internationally recognised certifications, a weak regulatory and supervisory framework, and weak framework for legal indemnities. There is poor management, plus poor staffing in terms of number and specialties of doctors and other healthcare providers. These have resulted in the low standard of care in the country.

---

[9]   International *Medical Travel Journal* (IMTJ), INDIA, NIGERIA: Increase in Nigerian Medical Tourism to India. November 2013.

This quote, no doubt, aptly captures the state of our healthcare system. Most people resident in the country will struggle to find a counter argument to this assessment. The bigger questions then are: What are the national targets for production of healthcare personnel? What is acceptable patient/healthcare personnel ratio? What is the quantum of spending on healthcare facilities across communities? What plans do we have for access to healthcare by all citizens?

Social Services

For the purpose of this chapter, we will look at social services as a range of public services provided by any national or state government agency for its residents, including such things as public housing and social security. Social security may also refer to the action programmes of government intended to promote the welfare of the population through assistance measures guaranteeing access to sufficient resources for food and shelter and to promote health and well-being for the population at large and potentially vulnerable segments such as children, the elderly, the sick and the unemployed. Services providing social security are often called social services.

Historically, because of the way society and governance evolved in Nigeria, social services, particularly social security, has been the purview of families and sometimes, friends. Government's role has been limited. However, with the increase in population, pervading poverty, income inequality and high rate of unemployment, this is an area where the government urgently needs to step in. The burden on families, of providing these services to loved ones, is simply unbearable in the face of diminishing resources. Having not done this traditionally, the government should focus on drivers for success such as an engagement methodology and reallocation of resources to address this need.

Infrastructure

The country remains challenged in terms of power, transportation and other physical infrastructure. Only recently has there been some attention to renewing some of the transportation infrastructure built by the colonial government and the military regimes of the 1970s. We are all too familiar with the current peak time generating capacity of about 4,517 megawatts when there is estimated latent demand of 19,000 to 20,000 megawatts. We will not moan much over this but will like to take the discourse to the direction of how our infrastructure deficit problem can be solved in an accelerated manner.

Good enough, a step has been taken in the right direction with the establishment of the Sovereign Wealth Fund with a seed investment of $1 billion and a clear mandate to invest part of these monies in infrastructural development. We need to take an additional step to ensure sustainability of this initiative by ensuring the funding mechanism is agreed on by all parties; federal, state and local governments. Needless to say that it is doubtful any meaningful greatness can be achieved with the current state of public infrastructure. The parlous state also has negative impacts on cost of doing business in Nigeria and support for domestic entrepreneurs.

Another potential source of funding for infrastructural development is the pension contribution by Nigerian citizens. The volume of contributions stands at ₦4.2 trillion as against a deficit of over ₦2 trillion in 2004. As it stands, the monies contributed so far can only be invested in government security and other money market instruments with a small proportion permitted to be invested in the stock market under very restrictive criteria. It is about time we put this money to real use in the provision of critical national infrastructure. We need to get the legislative and legal frameworks for this right. And government must step forward to provide some guarantees.

The Economy

A big challenge for the Nigerian economy is that it is a mono-product, commodity-based economy with oil as the major income earner. Nigeria has 36 states which are partially or wholly dependent on revenues from oil. Fiscal regime is weak as the country's tax revenue amounted to 6 percent of GDP, which is well below the 20 percent, consistent with developing countries without natural resources.[10]

---

[10]   FBN Capital Economic *Research, Economic Outlook*, October 2013

Nevertheless, over the years, sufficient income has accrued from oil and a bigger challenge has been the issue of proper management of resources and economic development.

A look at the most cited economic development indicators seem to tell a conflicting story, as it so often does especially in a developing country and commodity-based economy context. For Nigeria, while the GDP has recorded healthy growth rates in the last few years, it has not translated to better life nor impacted on our Human Development Indices. Life expectancy is 52 years and it ranks as the 17 lowest globally while 2013 literacy rate is put at 61 percent with a rank of 184 out of 194 countries.[11]

The National Bureau of Statistics (NBS) and the World Bank have also painted disturbing pictures of Nigeria's poverty dilemma. While NBS noted that about 112 million or 67 percent of total population lives below the poverty line, the World Bank in its "Nigeria Economic Report", notes that the number of Nigerians living in poverty is increasing rapidly. The report notes that "poverty rates remain high in Nigeria, particularly in rural areas".[12]

Two institutions, one national and the other international, have painted grim pictures about Nigeria's unemployment statistics in reports released in 2013. The National Population Commission notes that unemployment rate in Nigeria is 23.9 percent while the World Bank puts it at 25 percent but with a 38 percent youth unemployment rate. We believe these are statistics that should concern national and state economic managers because it has grave consequences for the future economy and security of the country.

Entrepreneurs, Enterprise and Innovation

Entrepreneurs and small enterprises drive every economy in the world, be it in the G7 countries, OECD (Organisation for Economic Cooperation and Development), BRICS (Brazil, Russia, India, China and South Africa) or ECOWAS (Economic Community of West

---

[11] World Country Facts, facts about Nigeria, November 2013.

[12] World Bank, Nigerian Economic Report, June 2013.

African States). This appears counter intuitive. But a quick back of the envelope calculation will illustrate. Diamond Bank employs a little over 10,000 Nigerians. Using that as an average for the industry, the 23 banks operating in the country employ about 230,000 Nigerians. Other sectors that are major employers include telecommunications, manufacturing and oil sectors. At the maximum, each would be at par with the banks. Perhaps, the largest employers will be the federal and state governments. Let us assume, for the sake of this argument, that they employ a further 8 to 10 million Nigerians, we would have accounted for employment status of somewhere around 11 million Nigerians. What about the rest of the Nigerians of working age (20-64 years old) estimated at 54 percent of the population of 168 million? What do the majority of these 90 million plus people do on a daily basis?

There are as many definitions of small and medium enterprises (SMEs) as there are countries. But there has been convergence on asset size, annual turnover and number of employees as key metrics for segmenting SMEs. In the European Union, 98 percent of the 19.3 million companies are categorised as SMEs and they provide 65 million jobs in member-countries.[13] SMEs also account for 66 percent of new jobs created in the European Union. In 2009, the International Finance Corporation put the annual market opportunity of SMEs in high and medium income countries at 40 percent of GDP.

In Nigeria, SMEs account for an estimated 91 percent of the number of companies and about 87 percent of total employment. SMEs contribution to GDP account for most of the growth witnessed in the past two years and such contributions were through agriculture, wholesale and retail trade, manufacturing, construction, hospitality, etc. These are the sectors in which the 90 million plus Nigerians mentioned earlier are engaged and make a living from, day after day, year after year. The companies they own are mostly micro, small and medium-scale enterprises and they operate in the grey economy, mostly ignored by national statisticians. More often than not, the crippling challenges that confront this segment are not only

---

[13] OECD SME and Entrepreneurship Outlook, Role of SMEs in the European Union, July 2005.

financial in nature but also border on such things as human resource limitations, access to markets, competitive-ness and creating business systems that work for today and are sustainable for future needs.

Fostering innovation is critical to success of not only individual entrepreneurs and companies, but also for business clusters that have emerged over time. In its simplest form, it could be the design and implementation of new processes in a company that reduces the cost of producing an existing product or service or it could be the development of a new product or service that creates new value for corporate and personal consumers. Thanks also to leading innovation thinkers, like Clayton Christensen, we now know that innovation, especially the disruptive type, is not limited to businesses but have proved to be very valuable in areas like education, healthcare delivery and governance. Entrepreneurs need to embrace innovation and be agents of innovation as that is a good long-term strategy to continue to be valuable to the market place.

Does government have a role in business? Yes, it does though opinions may differ. But one way government may meaningfully engage in business is by supporting industry clusters when these emerge, putting in place the right business support infrastructure and having the right administrative capacity, through the civil service, to run a system of governance that has the right incentives for businesses, and the right social infrastructure to attract the best people to live in the respective areas of jurisdiction. Is this the case in most states and the federal capital territory? Casual observation, personal and corporate experiences and the World Bank's "Doing Business in Nigeria 2013 report" incicate "No".

Civil Service

We mentioned the Civil Service briefly earlier to introduce the role it can play in creating a good business environment. Of course, the real role should go beyond that in any modern government. The Civil Service is the engine of any government. Its state of affairs, to a large extent, determines the successes recorded by incumbent administrations. It is one of those institutions which, in my opinion, should have been spared the scourge of quota system of employment, but should have been left to attract and retain the best people for careers there. Why is the Civil Service so important in governance? The following reasons immediately come to mind. The Civil Service

a. is responsible for the execution of laws promulgated by the government or legislated by the Legislature;
b. is in charge of administering all government services, social and business;
c. has charge of proposing expenditure heads under the annual budget cycle and ensuring monies are spent as appropriated;
d. plays a major role in determining priority investment areas to meet the needs of the populace.

The role of the Civil Service is well captured by Hem Chandra Pandit who notes:

> A relevant question concerns the extent to which the civil service is responsive, reliable, and responsible, as part of the government in a democratic regime. A responsive civil service caters more to the needs of the citizens than to its own tendencies to reproduce and grow. A reliable civil service delivers services that measure up to the standards of international economic competition and diplomacy and to the expectations of the democratic government in power as to the thorough implementation of its policies. A responsible civil service is held accountable by the majority of the electorate through the exercise of the right to vote and other forms of political participation. Furthermore, a responsible civil service refrains from discriminating against the parliamentary minority and against social groups who traditionally possess fewer resources, such as social status (racial or ethnic minorities) or political pull (women or the poor), than others.[14]

---

[14] Hem Chandra Pandit (2011). *Role of the Civil Service in a Democracy, Gender, Economy, Environment and Technology,*

If this onerous responsibility is to be discharged creditably, then a competent and effective Civil Service becomes a compelling case to ensure that only people with the right capacities, competence and character are employed or retained. Going a step further, civil servants should be rightly placed, i.e., putting square pegs in square holes. Doing otherwise will be to entrench a culture of incompetence as noted by Emile Faguet in his 1912 book, *The Cult of Incompetence*, which attacks successive French governments that ruined the Civil Service by a system of cronyism that appointed otherwise bright individuals into roles that they were not suited for either by reasons of education or past experiences.

The closing thoughts on the Civil Service are to acknowledge past attempts at some sort of reform, the latest being the one by the Oronsaye Committee. That these committees are set up in the first place is in recognition that there are problems. We now need to go beyond the reports submitted by the committees and act fast on the recommendations that are accepted. The journey to a great Civil Service will be a slow and painful process because bureaucracies do not change overnight. But start, we must!

Party Politics and Elections

Political party and elections in Nigeria have been more about personalities and ethnic orientation than any real political ideology of political parties and politicians. In the early 1990s, the two political parties that could not be identified with a dominant founder and financier, and were tagged a little to the left and a little to the right, the Social Democratic Party (SDP) and the National Republican Convention (NRC), respectively, were creations of the military government of the day. After the 1993 elections were annulled, the two political parties were dissolved.

The sometimes opaque ideology, if any, and deep-rooted ethnic focus are the bane of political party system and democracy in Nigeria. To date, no party has survived a military coup, and when democracy is reintroduced, we usually see most of the players gather in new associations with new names, with a new cohort made up of those you would have thought were ideological strange bedfellows with no common grounds. But again, maybe pragmatism about acquisition and use of power is what drives actions. Taking stock, however, this system of politics has ended up perpetuating individuals and leads to the quick succession of strong men, sometimes ill-equipped for governance, and not recognising their own shortcomings or inadequacies. There is a case for a system of party politics that is less dependent on individuals but more reliant on core beliefs and how governance should be approached. This we believe will strengthen our democracy and we need not go far to learn this lesson. Sierra Leone has two main parties, Sierra Leone Peoples Party (SLPP) founded in 1951 and All Peoples Congress (APC) founded in 1960. These two parties have at one time or the other dominated parliament and have survived three military coups (1967-1968), an attempt at a one-party state (1968-1971) and ten years of civil war (1991-2001). The current President of Sierra Leone was elected on the platform of the APC for a second term after succeeding a President who was elected on the platform of SLPP.

Take as another example, the African National Congress (ANC) founded in South Africa in 1912 and forced to remain underground for the greater part of her history up to 1994. The strength of its objectives and ideology kept it going even as it was not allowed to participate in elections for 84 years. Eventually, it won majority of seats in parliament and the presidential elections in 1994.

In our system, it is not uncommon to see an individual present his/her candidacy on up to three different political party platforms within one election cycle. There is no commitment to the party on the part of the individual, perhaps because there is also no commitment to fair play and a level playing field for individuals on the part of the party.

We also think that a stronger party system can lead to more credible elections even if it has been demonstrated that election management is not one of our national strengths. Aside from the 1993 election, no other election in the country has received universal acclaim as being free and fair. It is easy to make the usual mistake and attribute it to the change in electoral commission leadership, which before now seemed to change *enmass* after each election cycle. Luckily, in 2015, the same leadership in place in 2011, when the elections received some commendation, will be managing the elections again. Sadly, however, subsequent to 2011, especially in the senatorial by-elections in Delta State and the governorship election in Anambra State, the Independent National Electoral Commission (INEC) appears to have retrogressed and the old questions are being asked once again.

To have legitimacy and courage to carry out its programmes, a government must be seen to have come into power through an election that is free, fair and transparent. Short of that, the government will have legitimacy issues and will face crippling opposition from the citizens at large and even from within its own party. Most importantly, politics and credible elections are part determinants of the quality of governance or lack of it in the local governments, states or federation.

National Inflection Points

In differential calculus, an inflection point or point of inflection, is a point on a curve at which the curvature or concavity changes sign from plus to minus or from minus to plus. The curve changes from being concave upwards (positive curvature) to concave downwards (negative curvature), or vice versa.[15]

There are inflection points in our professional careers too: those moments where, due to events or new insights, everything is suddenly turned around or looks different in our choice of professions or the company/organisation we have chosen to work for. Often, they are mixed, bitter-sweet moments of self-understanding and emotional arrival.

In summary, an inflection point is an event that changes the way we think and act. There are also inflection points in a nation's history. For a nation, an event that results in a significant change in the economy, progress, geopolitical situation or mode of governance

---

[15]   http://mathworld.wolfram.com/InflectionPoint.htm

can be considered as an inflection point. It is a turning point after which a dramatic change, with either positive or negative outcomes, is expected to result in internal circumstances and conditions of countries, sub-regions and continents. Inflection points are more significant than the small day-to-day progress that is made and often with changes that are well-anticipated and widespread. Being able to realise positive or negative outcomes from inflection points depends on how we react to the event.

Nigeria has had her own fair share of inflection points since amalgamation in 1914. But the ones that easily come to mind, pre- and post-independence, are

1. Discovery of oil in commercial quantity in 1956;
2. Independence in 1960;
3. Referendum where parts of present Southern Cameroon opted to join the Cameroon federation rather than Nigeria in 1961;
4. The military coup d'état of 1966;
5. The 30-month civil war that started in 1967;
6. The oil price boom of the 1970s;
7. Subsequent military coups in 1975, 1976, 1983, 1985 and 1993;
8. Annulled presidential election of June 12, 1993;
9. Democratic governance that commenced in 1979 and 1999;
10. Multi-party elections from independence to date.

It is the countries endowed with the right leadership and institutions that can capitalise on inflection points that truly go on to become great nations. Countries whose situations were not materially different from Nigeria's in 1960, but who easily leveraged on inflection points, are

1. Singapore and her decision to opt out of the union with Malaysia;
2. Botswana which is made up of 70 percent desert and was one of the poorest countries in the world at independence in 1966;

3. South Korea, one of the poor Asian countries which split from North Korea in 1953 and endured months of war thereafter.

The list continues, ranging from countries all over the world which have successfully capitalised on inflection points.

Looking at some of our own inflection points highlighted above, it is our view that as a nation, we may have missed out on the real positives that could have accrued from the events. However, seeing that there are likely to be more inflection points in the future, even if few and far in between, the challenge for us is to determine how to capitalise on these in the future.

Before we conclude this section and without the benefit of hindsight, the following events that have recently occurred or may occur shortly will be good starting points to test frameworks for capitalising on inflection points:

1. The development and commercialisation of shale oil and gas by our major oil partners, which is a direct threat to our main income earner, crude oil and gas;
2. The proposed national dialogue, though the objective and timelines are still fuzzy;
3. The passage of the Petroleum Industry Bill into law;
4. The post-disposal management and regulation of Nigeria's power assets;
5. The 2015 general elections.

Fortunately, inflection points are not what we sit idly and wait to occur. They also include events we, as a nation and people, can catalyse.

Saving the Future

This chapter, luckily, is not about rehashing the woes that have befallen us as a nation. You are already familiar with these. It is about creating a new Nigeria that has bright prospects for future generations. Such a Nigeria, to put it in simple context, is a place where people would love to work and live, and a place where life and property is secure and governance works. How do we create such a country?

There are as many opinions as there are development experts and politicians as to how we can create such a country. We would like to add to the already long list so that the content of the debate and actions are enriched and robust.

The type of country we create in future will depend on, as as earlier pointed out, how we capitalise on inflection points on one hand, and the quantum and quality of investments we make in some of our national sectors today. The order of priority will determine how we allocate the monies available, to each sector. But keeping the order of priority on the sidelines, the following should attract focused attention from us:

Education

The three critical challenges that need to be addressed as far as education is concerned are funding, administration and curriculum. There is no reason why free top quality primary and secondary education cannot be offered by government to those who desire to be in public institutions. This will require that the state and local governments should vote substantial amounts in their annual budgets towards this. Additionally, there should be strict regulations for private operators of educational institutions at the primary and secondary levels of education to ensure adherence to pre-set standards and consistent quality across schools. Teaching methods should be dynamic and curriculum development should be continuous to ensure that the products of the system are well qualified for the higher levels of education and eventually life in general.

As for tertiary education, this is an area we need to rethink. Presently, apart from the private universities, it is funded fully by either states or the federal government. This system is not sustainable and in the past, it created the impression that tertiary education can be cheap. Tertiary education is not cheap and how we ran it in the past has had the cumulative effect of throwing out products that are without much education and are uncompetitive in the market place.

A system that might work will require interventions of both the public and private sectors and the co-operation of university unions and student bodies alike. The resistant points will be cost of attendance by students, a need by university administrators to generate non-school fee-based revenues, and more value-based research work by the faculty that can attract research funding on its own merit.

Social Welfare and Development

Wealthy nations spend a lot of money on social welfare while developing countries especially in Africa spend less. In the real sense of it, poverty is more endemic in the developing countries and this has excluded many of her citizens from such things as education, healthcare, food and shelter. As such, developing countries need to spend more of their annual budgets on welfare of their citizens. The current expenditure pattern has to do with the conundrum highlighted earlier in this chapter where governments are in a dilemma as to which public spending will cause development to happen faster: spending on social institutions and systems or on physical infrastructure.

The debate will continue for some time but what has proved to work is that an informed and knowledgeable, healthy populace with high self-esteem is likely to be a strong factor in economic development. Also, where a state is able to decisively address the issue of social services to the people, it tends to breed a more engaged and dedicated citizenship. It is also true that with better education and better skilled populace, reliance on social welfare will reduce drastically.

Governance

As citizens, we should constantly feel governance around us. This should reflect in our experiences and contacts with physical and social infrastructure. We should be confident that life and property are secured, and if we are involved in a dispute with third parties, we can seek redress and obtain justice from the courts. We need to test and validate that certain fundamental rights available to us as human beings are upheld by the government. We should be free from intimidation by state or private institutions and the state should also ensure we do not constitute a threat to others.

That should be the essence of governance. But having a system of governance that provides these guarantees is not a cheap proposition. It requires an active citizens/government collaboration and money, lots of money!

The revenue profile of over 80 percent of the states in the country indicates total dependence on revenues accruing to the Federation Account while for the country, over 80 percent of her revenue is dependent on the sale of crude oil. National and states economic managers need to be more creative, especially in the fiscal sense, in generating income to provide public services and invest in critical sectors. The right to tax is one of those areas that only a few states have explored effectively to increase their internally-generated revenue.

Governance does not come cheap. To make sure the bureaucracy that supports good governance is effective, we need to be dynamic in generating revenue and more dynamic in applying the revenues towards public good.

While acknowledging that governance is not cheap, it is conceded that we should do everything possible to reduce waste in cost of governance. Usually, we should ask ourselves how prudent it is to run a 36 state and 774 local government structure, each with its own bureaucracy. Add to that, 36 state governors, 36 state house of assembly, 774 local government chairmen and supporting councillors. In addition, remember that at the federal level, the President is obligated to appoint ministers from the 36 states, even when the nation does not have that number of ministries. In some cases, we have gone beyond that to also appoint complementary ministers from each geo-political zone.

It is with the knowledge of these facts that we have perennial demand for more states by the citizenry. So far, state creation has led to the balkanisation of existing territory within Nigeria's boarder.

This is different from the American example, so often quoted, where the American government purchased land masses from France and other countries to add to the American federation and grow the number of states from the initial 13 colonies at independence to 50 states today. The pertinent question to ask is: "In the face of dwindling national resources, do we need to pander to ethnic and primordial considerations that will only serve to drive up level of cost and attendant waste in our system?"

Another matter that should be addressed is the issue of representation at the federal legislature with the Senate as case study. As it stands, every state in the federation is represented by three senators regardless of physical size or population. In the Second Republic, it was five senators per state, though we had only 19 states then. Is this equitable? These are issues of governance that are expected to receive priority attention from economic managers as we seek to build a more appealing future for our children.

Physical Infrastructure

The quantum and quality of investment we make in our public infrastructure is critical to the country we will have tomorrow. Having already fallen behind in the provision of modern public infrastructure, the magnitude of spending required to catch up is now mind boggling.

The state of infrastructure, in a way, has a bearing on the size of domestic and external investment that a country can attract. So, when the usual arguments about the levels of foreign investment coming into the country are presented, much of it hot money by the way, one usually wonders what it would have been if we had the right infrastructure in place.

In the next few years, we should spend considerable part of our budgets on providing the requisite infrastructure. The spending pattern on recent budgets, where an average of 28 percent and 31 percent of total budgets were proposed for capital expenditure in 2012 and 2013, respectively, does not acknowledge the magnitude of infrastructure deficit. We also need to see a more productive engagement of the private sector through private-public partnership models that have proven to work elsewhere, within the right legal framework that provides protection for capital injection by the private sector.

In the next few years, it is suggested that the government should define its capital spending priorities and investment drives to attract funding for our interstate and city roads, railways, bridges, airports, shipping ports, urban renewal, portable water systems, power generation, distribution and transmission, airports, etc.

National Competitiveness

> Nations compete to offer the most productive environment for business. Competitiveness depends on the productivity, with which a nation uses its human, capital, and natural resources.[16]

National competitiveness can be viewed from two perspectives. The first, as defined by Porter above, where Nigeria, as a country competes for domestic and foreign investments by offering the most productive environment for capital, and the second is how the products and services that originate from Nigeria are able to compete with those offered by the rest of the world. Whatever perspective of national competitiveness we take, there is a primary role for government. The paper referred to above did identify determinants of national competitiveness and are listed as follows:

a. Quality of the national business environment;
b. State of cluster development;
c. Sophistication of company operations and strategy;
d. Social infrastructure and political institutions;
e. Macroeconomic policies

---

[16]   Michael Porter (2009). *Creating a competitive Nigeria: Towards a shared Economic Vision*, July.

At the bottom of the pile is natural endowment which is well enough because with the absence of counter examples, the tendency is to believe that resource rich countries are the most competitive. Let us remember Israel, Singapore and Switzerland, who are all lacking in any form of natural resource.

Natural resource, however, does create an advantage if well harnessed in the sense that it creates platforms of ready-made business clusters to build on. But on its own, it presents no clear advantage. In the past, the nation had business clusters in different regions, especially in leather, textile, shoes, groundnuts, etc. But our inability to sustain the cycle of investments, organisation, harnessing and reinvestment in cluster infrastructure has led to their quick demise.

Sophistication of company operations and strategy is another factor we have not touched much here. In summary, it is what determines the national and international desirability and demand for the goods and services produced in the country. However, Nigeria was ranked 147 out of 189 countries surveyed in ease of doing business.[17] It recorded very low ratings in areas such as getting electricity, registering property, trading across borders, enforcing contracts and paying taxes. It is difficult to do business here. These are simple fact. The products and services that come out of this system will struggle to compete in quality or, if it is the right quality, will struggle to compete on price.

These are just some of the areas we need to pay closer attention to in order to build a competitive and more attractive country in the future. It is not about the government alone. It is also about a citizenry that is involved in the process, paying their taxes and holding the government accountable to its responsibilities to them.

Now and then, one recalls an article, written about an expatriate on his first trip to China, probably in the late 1970s, and astonished at the pace of work and commitment of the people and government

---

[17]   World Bank (2013). *Ease of Doing Business Report: Nigeria.*

to building a modern society. He asks his tour guide if they ever took things easy in China. She explained to him that the current generation could not afford to do that having inherited from the previous generations, a country that was poor. They were now saddled with building a better country for the future generations and as such, most people saw themselves as the generation of sacrifice. That perhaps is how we need to view our role in saving the future.

Bibliography

Achebe, Chinua, *The Trouble with Nigeria* (Heinemann Books, 1984; Fourth Dimension Publishing Co., 2000); *Things Fall Apart* (Heinemann Books, 1958).

Ajanaku, Lucas, in an article in *Tell* magazine (2008).

Akinlua Akinsola, *Driving curriculum content and practice in higher education in Nigeria towards relevance, Reforming Higher education in Africa.*

Angerou, Chrisanthi, Discourses *on Innovation and Development in Information Systems in Developing Countries*

Badal, S, (2010) *How large corporations can spur small business growth.*

Cantor, Norman F., describes how, in the late medieval period, coal was the new alternative fuel

Castells, M., *The Information Age: Economy, Society and Culture.*

China Business Survey (2013)

Dauda, R.O., *Investment in Education and Economic Growth in Nigeria: A Co-integration Approach.*

Eklund, Ken *et al*, *World Without Oil* (WWO, 2007) a television game series on the Independent Television Service (ITS).

Emerging Markets Spotlight

Eze, Paul, On corruption in Nigeria (2012).

Ezekwesili, Oby, An address delivered as the Guest Speaker at the National Summit of the All Progressives Congress (APC) in Abuja on March 6, (2014).

Faguet, Emile: *The Cult of Incompetence* (1912).

FBN Capital Economic Research, Economic Outlook, October 2013.

Gjersø, J.F., "A Nigerian Oil Curse," in *The Civilising Mission* (30th April, 2010)

Hanushek, E.A, Wobmann, L, *Education quality and economic growth,* World Bank (2007).

Huerta, Ignacio Palacious & Acemoglu, Daron (eds). "The World our grandchildren will inherit", in *100 Years: Leading Economists Predict the Future,* (MIT, 2013).

International Medical Travel Journal (IMTJ), INDIA, NIGERIA: Increase in Nigerian Medical Tourism to India (November 2013).

Liu, Y "Development of Private Entrepreneurship in China: *Process, Problems and Countermeasures", in Entrepreneurship in Asia: Playbook for Prosperity (CD publication by the Maureen and Mike Mansfield Foundation Program)* (2003).

Marx, Karl, On history.

Maslow, A, "A Theory of Needs." In *Psychological Review,* 1943.

Millennium Development Goals (MDGs), Target on Education.

Morales-Gomez and Melesse Sahlfeld, in a review of how ICTs work for development.

Nigeria: A Country Study, Washington: GPO for the Library of Congress, (1991).

Nzeogwu, Chukwuma, K., Military Coup Speech, 1966.

OECD SME and Entrepreneurship Outlook, Role of SMEs in the European Union (July 2005).

Onwenu, Onyeka, Nigeria: *A Squandering of Riches* (a television documentary).

Pandit, Hem Chandra, Role of the Civil Service in a Democracy, Gender, Economy, Environment and Technology (2011).

Porter, Michael, *Creating a competitive Nigeria: Towards a shared Economic Vision* (July 2009).

Shakespeare, William: *As You Like It*

Shell Petroleum Development Corporation (SPDC, 2013). LIVE Wire programme.

Siollun, Max, *Oil Politics and Violence – Nigeria's Military Coup culture (1966-1976),* Algora Publishing (2009).

The Centre for Solar Energy and Hydrogen Research at Baden-Württemberg and the Fraunhofer Society in Germany.

The CIA World Fact-book.

The corruption perception index (2013)

The Federal Inland Revenue Services (FIRS, 2008).

The Federal Ministry of Education (FME), Annual Report (2012).

The International Energy Annual (EIA), Nigeria's oil production and consumption (1980-2005).

The Land Use Act, 1978.

The Manufacturers' Association of Nigeria (MAN, 2012).

The National Bureau of Statistics (NBS) Report 2013.

The Nigerian Association of Chambers of Commerce, Industry, Mines and Agriculture (NACCIMA), statement by the Director General at the time, Dr. John Isemede (February 2013).

The Nigerian Communication Commissions: *FIGURES*.

The report released by New York-based The Revenue Watch Institute (RWI), The Resource Governance Index (May 2013).

The Revenue Watch Institute of the Open Society Foundations, a report on Nigeria's performance on the *Resource Governance Index*

The United Nations Development Programme (UNDP) 2001 Report.

The World Bank Report 1989, 2012)

The World Bank, Ease of Doing Business Report: Nigeria (2013).

The World Bank, Nigerian Economic Report (June 2013).

Transparency International *Corruption Perception Index* (2013).

Udo Udo-Aka, My Journey: *As the future becomes the past*, May-Five Media, 2014.

UNESCO, Education for All (EFA) Report (2011).

United States Census Bureau (2009).

United States Embassy in Nigeria, Education Section, Nigerian Education Fact Sheet (2012).

Wikipedia, Profile on the Nigerian petroleum industry, extracted in (February 2014).

World Country Facts (Facts about Nigeria, November 2013).

Index

www.ingramcontent.com/pod-product-compliance
Lightning Source LLC
Chambersburg PA
CBHW021541200526
45163CB00014B/362